CW00858295

The Primates of IIT
ISBN-10: 1468053612
ISBN-13: 978-1468053616

The Primates

of

IIT

Kanpur: 1972-77

Editors: M. S. Madhukar and M. Arora

Date of Publication: February 3, 2012

Edited by: *M. S. Madhukar and M. Arora*

Cover Design: *M. S. Madhukar and M. Arora*

Inside Illustrations: *Nigel Rogers*

DEDICATED

To the Batch of 1972-77, IIT Kanpur

PREFACE

Most of us have done things during our teen years which when we reminisce, we often say 'how could we?', and which we hope and pray now that our children will never do. The idea of putting these things in print precipitated from a casual conversation between two of us. When the idea was floated to the rest of the group, it had a snowball effect with many of us enthusiastic to share their episodes that they had kept under wraps till now. Some of these episodes just happened to us while in others we were just looking for trouble. Not only that each one of these happenings captures a particular moment during our stay at IIT/K, they reveal something about each of us – our wild sides, experiences, frustrations, imperfections, rawness, childishness, simplicity, adventures, immaturity, and most of all our stupidities.

Out of a concern to those of us whose episodes contain material which might raise some eyebrows, we have concealed the names of the main characters. We also received some stories that were too revealing and beyond the liberal rating meters of this book. Those stories are kept out of this book and will be shared only with an exclusive audience during our 35th year reunion.

The *Introduction* is an article written by one of the batch mates, David Thomas, which captures the glimpse of the socioeconomic and political climate of that period. The chapters following the *Introduction* are random collection of episodes contributed by some of our 'brave' batch mates.

Please use discretion in revealing the real names of the characters in some of the stories to an audience outside our own batch.

Contributors

Arun Goel

Barid Mitra

Chandan Das

David Thomas

Hemant Jalan

K.K. Shukla

M.S. Madhukar

Mohan Arora

Mukesh Anjaria

Nirmal Jha

Ramesh Mahadevan

Renu Mehrotra

Sanjiv Vashisht

Vikas Chandra

Vipul Agarwal

x

CONTENT

Acknowledgement

To all our batch mates particularly those of us who have refused to grow up and are proud to admit that once upon a time we were less stupid than what we are today.

Introduction: It was just yesterday

We joined IITK in 1972 when the nation was collectively on a high. Just six months earlier in December 1971, Bangladesh had been liberated and India was ruled by the imperious Indira Gandhi, then at the height of her might and majesty. She had won the 5th Lok Sabha elections in 1971 with a thumping majority, her Congress party winning an impressive 352 seats, leaving just 22 for the Jan Sangh, the earlier avatar of the BJP. Indira had won with a powerful, simple message, 'गरीबी हटाओ' which resonated with the poor. (Never mind that 35 years later Garibi is still to be hataoed). They thronged the polling booths to vote for her, their slogan being, 'ना जात पे ना पात पे, बस इन्दिरा जी की बात पे, मोहर लगेगी हाथ पे.' Indira was not just the tallest among leaders, she was the only leader, the others being merely her retainers. Among these retainers was the colourless Kamlapathi Tripathi who was the Chief Minister of UP when we joined IITK. Another retainer was V V Giri who was the President of our country when we first took the dusty road from Kanpur Central to Kalyanpur.

As the poet said, 'We were young, we were merry, we were very, very wise...' We knew a lot - or thought we did - and were interested in a whole range of subjects but I don't remember politics or society being among them. We read Western and Indian philosophy but not Karl Marx or Adam Smith. We discussed Herman Hesse and Somerset Maugham but not Gandhi, Nehru or Lohia. We were, to a large extent, blissfully unaware and

1

unconcerned about the historical milieu in which we found ourselves. We were caught up in ourselves, our studies and our lives.

Many of us, though, did take the trouble to attend the IITK MP Lectures or listen to other public figures visiting the campus. But it was with the natural curiosity that comes to the young than due to any troubled social consciousness. We gave a standing ovation to Subramanium Swamy when he spoke about the economic and political stagnation of India and exhorted us to take a year off to join the movement for change. We listened attentively when Piloo Mody gave us his cynical observation about the Nehru family but were not so attentive when Jayprakash Narayan told us that as students of Technology we needed to take a special interest in gobar gas plants. Even Mohit Sen of the CPI impressed us with his clarity of thought. Morarji Desai and L K Advani too spoke to us but for the life of me I can't remember what they said. Clearly they did not leave an impression.

It seems to me that in those days we were less conscious of caste and religion than students are today. We divided students into groups of muggus, fathrus etc. and maybe even into regional groups – the Jam gang, the Southie gang, the Lucknow gang etc. but rarely did we look on students as being Hindu, Christian, Muslim, forward, backward, Dalit and so on. If at all there was a divide it was between the more urban, English speaking students and the more rural Hindi speakers but there were innumerable friendships across the divide and the divide itself seemed to level out towards the end of our five years at IITK.

So then, what did we notice about the world around us. We noticed that a girl called Karen Lunel looked stunning in a green bikini in the first Liril advertisements. We read with interest Kushwant Singh's Illustrated Weekly, Desmond Doig's Junior Statesman or JS and Anees Jung's Youth Times. We looked up when India Today was launched in 1975 and Sunday by M J Akbar in 1976. Shobha De nee Kilachand made Stardust famous during our heydays. Our reading habits can also be judged from the fact that there was a copy of Debonair or a Nick Carter sizzler under many pillows in the rooms in Hall Three.

If we chose to read poetry, which very few of us did, the poets of the day were Kamala Das and Pritish Nandy. Many of us thought we could write and found outlets for our creative efforts, such as they were, in the Spark, Counterpoint, Cheshire Cat and even the campus NCC bulletin which was called 'The Cadet News'.

We listened more to Vividh Bharati than watched the only television channel, the black and white Doordarshan. Our toothpaste was Binaca, our detergent was Det, our shaving cream was Palmolive (some of us did not need to shave and some of us would not) and if we had a radio, it was a Murphy.

And then there was cinema. Our stay at IITK coincided with arguably the best years of Hindi cinema. In 1973 we drooled over Dimple Kapadia in Bobby. From 1975 onwards it was the angry young man of Hindi cinema, Amitabh Bachchan who had us in thrall. Deewar, Zanzeer, Pakeezah, Amar Akbar Antony and the granddaddy of them all – Sholay And the leading ladies who occupied our many sleepless nights – Hema Malini, Parveen Babi, Zeenat Aman and Neetu Singh – can one ever forget their sensuousness, even if one now finds their chiffon sarees, their transparent sleeves, tight kurtis, straight hair and flowers a little quaint.

Alternate cinema for us and the SFS meant the occasional Czech or Polish film with its few scenes of semi nudity. We were as animal as could be in our appreciation, healthily animal.

L7 when SFS films were screened with an 8mm projector was the crucible where a part of our outlook on life was formed. There we were as politically and socially incorrect as possible. We invented interactive cinema. Watching Helen dance her 'पिया तू' number in the third 'repeat' in smoke filled L7 was what made life worth living.

We wore trousers of all fits and shapes and shirts in every hue of the rainbow. Our footwear was normally just slippers. All our clothes were ill fitting. For the few of us who were fashion conscious, Bell bottoms and shirts with large collars were thought to be the height of fashion. V C Shukla, the Information Minister was thought to be nattily dressed in his safari suit but who cared.

On the few occasions when we looked at the outside world, we noticed that the Prime Minister's son, a certain Sanjay Gandhi, had formed a company called Maruti Udyog to manufacture cars although till we left

3

IITK, not a single Maruti car hit Indian roads. The India economy was small, controlled and inward looking. India's total exports in 1975 were 4036 crore rupees. Today, a single company, Infosys, does better than that. When we were at IITK, five and ten paise coins still jingled in our pockets and we could get our slippers repaired by Gangu mochi for the princely sum of twenty five paise. Petrol was Rs. 3 a litre and a cinema ticket cost all of two rupees. The official wage rate for part time student employment at IITK was two rupees an hour.

Computerisation was unknown and every time I had to book a train ticket to my home in Delhi I had to go to the Kanpur railway station, fill out a long form, stand in a longer queue and finally watch the clerk at the counter enter my reservation in a thick, large ledger. If I did not get a reserved ticket, I had to travel in a packed, unreserved second class compartment were the seats were uncushioned and even the toilet was crammed full with sitting passengers. The only consolation was steaming hot tea in a matka at Etawah or Hathras.

The late sixties and early seventies were the salad days of the hippie culture worldwide. We watched at a distance – fascinated at these people from another world. Zeenat Aman brought us that culture second hand in दम मारो दम. I got to watch a little more of that culture at rather closer quarters when, after attending a TELCO job interview at Pune (I was not selected if you really must know), I traveled to Goa and spent a couple of days at Anjuna Beach – wide eyed !

Then as now, cricket was the national pastime. Cricket was brought to us on All India Radio by the likes of Dicky Rutnagar and Pearson Surita. Those were the glory days of spin – of our famed quartet – Bedi, Prassana, Chandrashekhar and Venkatraghavan. A certain young man called Sunil Gavaskar was just beginning to make his mark. Then, as now, the team selection was questionable and erratic. In 1974-75 when the Indians toured the West Indies, Venkatraghavan was made the captain for one test and then in the next he did not find a place in the team at all!

The outside world – India's politics and society rarely intruded into IITK. Probably less than ten percent of us followed political developments. In late 1973, students in Gujarat launched the Nav Nirman movement against corruption and for change in society. There were violent clashes which subsided only when the Chief Minister of Gujarat, Chimanbhai Patel resigned and the assembly was dissolved. We barely noticed.

We were more concerned with our Students Gymkhana politics. Elections were contested hotly and the issues were mostly apolitical although there was a left wing group on campus headed by the likes of Swapan Lahiri, PK Singh and Joey Raghavan ably assisted by Professors A. P. Shukla and Sahasrabudhe. Similarly there was a right wing lobby centered around RSS activists led by R. K. Bansal and Pawan Kumar and guided by Professors Dhoopar and Oberoi.

Students Gymkhana Presidents were colourful personalities. In our time we had Ricky Surie, Radha Pillai, Mac Pillai, Rakesh Bhan and finally our very own Sanjiv Sahay. Predating Anna Hazare by 34 years, the Gymkhana Office bearers - Sanjiv Sahay, Hemant Jalan, Jai Shankar Sharma and I - went on a one day hunger strike in 1977 to urge the acting Director, J N Kapoor, to intervene to solve the problems in the Hall 2 mess.

Throughout 1974 and early 1975, we did notice that there were a number of agitations and discontent across the country. Indira Gandhi's Bangladesh halo was beginning to fade. Jayprakash Narayan had launched his Sampoorna Kranti Andolan and students joined his movement in large numbers particularly in Bihar. Even in IITK there were a few discussions and lectures on JP's Sampoorna Kranti.

The country was ruled by Indira Gandhi's yes men. Fakhrudin Ali Ahmed became President and N. D. Tewari became the Chief Minister of Uttar Pradesh. Yes, the very same N. D. Tewari of 'ना हूं नर, ना हूं नारी, मैं हूं N. D. Tewari' fame. (Maybe this slogan can be used by defense lawyers in the ongoing paternity suit against N. D. Tewari).

And then came, the bombshell. On 12th June 1975, the Allahabad High Court set aside Indira Gandhi's election on technical charges of impropriety in the 1971 elections. The country waited with bated breath for Indira Gandhi's reaction. It did not have long to wait. On 25th June, the President declared emergency in the country and that gave Indira Gandhi the power to rule by decree. There were mass arrests across the country. At IITK both Prof. Dhoopar on the right and Prof. A. P. Shukla on the left were arrested. Prof. H. S. Mani had to take Prof. Shukla's classes. Exams were postponed and held only after the summer break.

But sadly at IITK, protests against the emergency were muted. Most students were unaware of the larger issues involved and we continued to live our normal student lives. When the journalist Inder Malhotra wrote 'not a dog barked' referring to the reaction to the declaration of emergency, he was talking about India but he could have been talking specifically about IITK. During the emergency, not one student at IITK was arrested - a dubious distinction which very few colleges in North India had.

Student Union elections were banned across the country. Our own Student Gymkhana elections were also banned initially but later the Director, Amitabh Bhattacharya, managed to get a waiver and elections were held. IITK was probably the only college in India where elections were held during the emergency, another pointer to our docility.

We could not help noticing though that for a short period of time Kishore Kumar was banned from All India Radio. It was said in hushed tones that he had refused to sing at a Youth Congress rally and had therefore been summarily taken of the air by Sanjay Gandhi.

In the country at large, 1976 was best known for the family planning program ruthlessly driven by Sanjay Gandhi. Any man with two children or more had to compulsorily be sterilised. Local officers were given sterilisation targets and in order to meet them even the old, the very young, petty offenders and vagrants were rounded up. The fear of 'Nasbandi' was very real. There were unconfirmed reports that even seventy year old Gangu mochi had been 'nasbandified'!

And then suddenly on March 21st 1977 at the fag end of our IITK days the emergency was lifted and elections were called. The Students Senate, quiet as a mouse during the emergency (some individual senators did mutedly protest), now passed a resolution welcoming its end. In its inimitable, humbug soaked style, characteristic of the campus left, the resolution began, 'The Students Senate hails the release of political prisoners and the end of totalitarian rule in the country.'

Some of us traveled to Delhi to be among the lakhs who thronged Ramlila maidan to listen to JP, Jagjivan Ram and a host of others. The

Janata Dal swept the polls across the country or at least the Northern part of it. The country celebrated, spoons were used to clang in celebration in the Hall 1 mess as the results came in and a midnight procession was taken to the Director's house. The final tally – Janata Dal 298, Congress 153 – and the stern, principled, urine drinking Gandhian, Morarji Desai, became our next Prime Minister.

And soon after the end of the emergency came the end of our stay at IITK. An eventful five years came to an end. We were witnesses to history in the making – or were we? We were probably too busy, dividing our time between cramming for the end semesters and watching Zeenie Baby in L7.

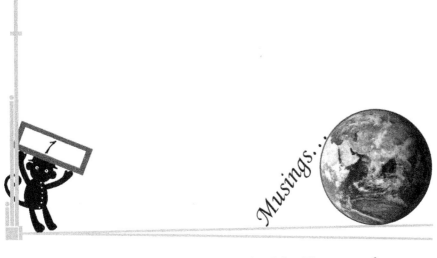

At our freshers nite sometime in July 72 some of us were pitchforked onto the stage in our underpants ala '3 Idiots'. I remember Paul Tapsall, Hemant Jalan, MS Narayan competing for the Miss Fresher title. The winner was Paul with his soft long hair & chiseled features. I was also one of the dancers on stage trying to bare my non existent muscles.

Ranga, Kamath, Prateek were some of the raggers –in-chiefs. We were made to do the Phantom act where underpants were worn on top of our trousers. I was frequently banished to IIT Shimla – a euphemism for perching on top of the built in wardrobes. On one occasion I was actually made to sit inside the wardrobe and keep opening the door to announce the offer of my posterior to any takers. I felt like a cuckoo imprisoned in a Swiss cuckoo clock.

We had a freshers TT tournament in Hall 3. Top contenders were Pradeep Agnihotri, David Thomas and I. Pradeep beat me in the finals and I became the 'runners up', a nickname that stuck for a long time. Later on I was up for selection to the IIT team and was granted access to the Hall V TT room to play with the then legends like Ronak Shodhan, Ashwini Chadha. Sporting facilities on campus were marvellous with very few takers.

Playing cricket for IITK was a thrilling experience. I remember captains like Anoop Bais, Rahul Mukherjee, Partha Bannerjee and our very own 'Bugger' Santanu Mukherjee. We had a M. Tech. Services Ranji player called K.K. Rao who was a great all rounder. The team visited BITS Pilani for Oasis 76 – a cultural and sporting extravaganza in the desert. Playing on a cold wintry morning on a matting wicket, I was able to get the early breakthrough which helped us to win the match. Playing in the Kanpur league, Inter year tournaments and ofcourse inter wing tennis ball matches was great fun and allowed us the much needed respite from quizzes, relative grades and frequent bouts of depression . IITK was a great leveller with school rankers and state toppers finding themselves all at sea with Advanced Engineering Maths, Fluid Mechanics and even the physical sciences.

We had a suicide almost every semester and even the presence of an attractive lady counsellor like Mrs. Usha Kumar in her Volkswagen, could do very little to stem the tide. The tough academic environment needed us to toughen ourselves to brace the onslaught. My first year grades were predictably disastrous. Gradually I learnt to cope and beat the system and grades in subsequent years actually improved. Later on as we prepared ourselves for placements, I discovered to my pleasant surprise that soft skills and all round abilities also had an important role to play in job interviews. I wish I could have extracted more from the IIT Campus Experience!

The Annual cultural festival now called Antaragni was a much looked forward to event. Hordes of city slickers and beautiful babes descended on campus, leaving us starry eyed. It was also the era of feminist activism inspired by the likes of Germaine Greer and movements like 'burn the bra'. I remember the stunning presence of a participant from Miranda House that left very little to the imagination of our young and fertile minds.

There was a scramble to become volunteers to chaperone the girls teams from Loreto Kolkata, Lucknow & LSR and Miranda House from Delhi University. The volunteers strutted around like peacocks much to the chagrin of their less fortunate batchmates. The few IIT girls on campus were completely upstaged by their more attractive species.

During our first year, some of us like Neeraj Nityanand, Sekhar, Ajai Mathur & I opted to get involved with dramatics too. We put up a play called 'Night at an Inn' by Lord Dunsany where I had to play the part of a drunken sailor. At one point in in play, as I lay on stage, Ajai emptied some real rum into my mouth to get me to feel more natural. A second play by the name of 'Jhumritalaiya Mein Suar' starring Mohan Arora, Lalit Gulati saw some memorable rehearsals being conducted behind closed doors. I suspect the censoring authorities would never have allowed a public screening of this play. My tryst with theatre got me involved with backstage expertise like props, sound and lights – something that kept me on stage for all dramatics events at festivals. I remember handling backstage for a play called the 'Puny Little Life Show' that we performed at Kanpur City. The cast was from the 76 batch – Sudhakar Kesavan, Tridib Sen & Ranjan Kaul.

During our second year, we were licenced to Rag the 78 batch. This was a very bright batch with several 5 pointers from ISC like Srikant Garde, Christopher Flores, Peter Varman etc. All these guys with some smart Dosco's and Columbum's were confronted with Kanpuria speak – What is IIT in shudh Hindi? Bhartiya Takniki Sansthan right. Wrong, much worse! What is a four letter word ending in UNT & distinctly feminine, *UNT Right. Wrong, it's AUNT you dirty minds. An innocent fresher stammered that he knew it was a TOOL of a dame!

Watching movies at L7 was a much looked forward to weekend pursuit. We all ran to grab the best seats, played bridge till the screening began, and forced rewinds for the exciting cabaret scences. Now these have

been replaced by item numbers. We also went to town for some new releases and turned on the Angrezi Charm at the manager's office at Heer Palace to get out of turn tickets. The tempo rides from Bada Chowraha to AYAYTee Kalyanpur were memorable. I have variously sat on the mudguard, stepney, window of the Tempo. At Green Park, we had a separate IIT enclosure in the students pavilion and it was a treat to watch G R Viswanath scoring a 100 against New Zealand in rapidly fading light.

The fond memories of IITK would be incomplete without a word about my roommate and wingmates with whom we grew up. Jai Sekhar from St Josephs Dehradun was my roommate – unkempt, untidy but a live wire. Changed his Branch from Chemical to Metallurgical and came out on top! Is today a successful Professor-Researcher-Entrepreneur-Speaker based at Cincinatti? Lalit Gulati and Subroto Basu from St Francis Lucknow were our immediate neighbours. Lalit, Subroto & I were Mech. Lalit studied the least, disturbed others the most and did the best. I had the last laugh when our final year project grades were announced. Despite doing most of the work, Subroto & Lalit barely scraped through & I got a 'B' thanks to the perception of a certain Prof B P Singh in whose course I had done surprisingly well. Lalit is a management consultant having had successful stints with Citi, Accenture, and Cadburys. He lives in Texas. Subroto is with GE Aircraft Engines at Cincinatti. MS Narayan & Pammy Singh from Kanpur were next. They were generally horizontal during day and night. MS used to read with his book on the floor and his head perched on the edge of his bed. He now lives in Australia. Pammy joined the IAS, Gujarat cadre and seems to be on an overseas sabbatical. Then there were the Bhargava cousins Prabhat & Akhilesh, Santanu Mukherjee & 'Saheb Bahadur' Khare. We also had Shakul Rai, Sanjay Singh & Aftabur Rahman. Sanjay is a colleague at ITC and runs our Paper business. Aftabur was a good natured Bihari & the butt of many pranks. On one occasion, Jai got him to dress up for an interview for the position on the Board of Governors of IITK.

Checking out of IITK in 1977 was difficult. It was home for 5 years and made us men from boys. Personally speaking, I have benefitted immensely from the IIT system at highly subsidized costs. I am now an active evangelist for the Pan IIT Alumni Movement which is involved with a host of Nation Building Projects.

You know you're over fifty, if ...

Your latest reading includes 'Windows Vista for DUMMIES'

Cricket team की माँ की...

The incident took place during our first mid-semester exams of 3rd year, first semester. I distinctly remember that it was Jitendra Gupta who started it all, screaming howlers from Wing 6 across to Wing 1, in an attempt to digest whatever he could not comprehend about Fluid Mechanics or some other obscure subject. He went solo for a good 5-10 minutes, before guys from our Wing 1 responded, and by some magic, everyone was out in the corridors in no time, shouting at each other. This was quite normal, and nothing particular to recall after 35 years, except for what happened thereafter.

There was a cricket tournament of school kids going on at IITK then, and school-kids were housed both in the TT rooms of Hall 3 and Hall 2. The kids had a nightmare when they heard the sudden burst of noise at an ungodly hour (for them) of 11 pm, and they all trooped out into the quadrangle in their pyjamas. By then, we had all got pretty tired of screaming गाली at each other, and the attention shifted to these hapless kids: "Cricket team की माँ की....." rendered the air. Poor fellows. They ran helter skelter and called up the warden (as they had probably been instructed to do so in the event of earthquakes and other calamities).

By then a collective decision had already been taken to march to Hall 2, which everyone did spontaneously. After the usual letting off steam once we reached there, the frightened 1st year batch that was housed in

Hall 2 ran (most of them) towards Jaggu Market to save their skins. In another 30 minutes we were quite satiated, and started our retreat march, when it was reported that the Hall 2 warden (Dr. R. D. Srivastava alias Tarzan) had arrived, and had seized two of the 2nd year students from Hall 3 who were lagging behind. This infuriated us, and we trooped back from the tennis courts to Hall 2, and confronted Tarzan.

He had locked up the two 2nd year blokes in the warden's room, and refused to budge. Our Prof Singh (i.e. Ashok Kumar Singh) threatened Tarzan that what he had done "constituted an illegal detention of minors", as the two boys in question were not yet 18 years of age. We roared in approval, but Tarzan was not ruffled. Meanwhile the Gymkhana President Mac Pillai arrived, with other Gymkhana officials in tow, to start negotiations with Tarzan to retrieve possession of the two boys. We were told to disperse, but our hearts were still there. I remember at that time, Jainagesh Sekhar and myself got the bright idea of telephoning the Health Centre and requesting that an ambulance and stretcher be sent for Dr. R. D. Srivastava! While delicate negotiations for the freedom of two students were in progress, the stretcher arrived, and the men announced that they had come to carry away Dr. R. D. Srivastava. Tarzan hit the roof on hearing this, and all negotiations were scuttled.

The incident ended a few days later with the resignation of Wardens of Hall 3 (D. Balasubramaniam) and Hall 2 (Tarzan).

You know you're over fifty, if ...

You still find Hema Malini, Zeenat Aman, Rekha, Dimple Kapadia cute.

That's my ten!

From one of Jitendra Gupta's emails to me, I learnt that Tekedar, the dimunitive, grumpy and somewhat wacko mess worker of Hall III had passed away. (I guess, years of eating Hall III mess grub can do it to you) To me, Tekedar was as much a part of my IIT K landscape as the SFS movies or CNR Rao lectures or the canteen chow miens. Let me narrate a Tekedar story, as told by K. S. Balaji of our batch.

Remember those days we used to suffer from chronic cash flow problems? Remember those days when our parents used to be irrationally tight-fisted about doling us money? Remember how Neeraj Nityanand used to double-padlock all his belongings? In those trying economic times, Balaji had evolved into a महा कंजूस, probably falling in the three sigma of the population. During one of his weak moments however, Tekedar approached him and subjected him to a sob story and finagled a soft loan of ten rupees, with a 'कल लौटा दूंगा' promise. The next day came and Balaji being Balaji, promptly asked for his money. And Tekedar being Tekedar, came up with a typical 'अरे साहब, मैं आपको देने वाला था, लेकिन मेरा भाई बीमार हो गया....' kind of story. This went on for several more days – Balaji hassling him and Tekedar sliming away. Finally, a few weeks later, Balaji simply gave up, becoming a wiser man.

Fast forward a few more weeks. Suddenly someone was talking about a big marriage in one of the villages nearby with नौटंकी and nautch girls. We all rushed over. Sure enough there was a massive crowd and a

16

skimpily clad, terrible looking woman was gyrating away to old Asha Bhonsle tunes. We rubbed shoulders with the village crowd to gawk. At the end of a particularly sexy number, people started hurling money at her and a ten rupee note that came flying toward her was actually lobbed by none other than Tekedar. Balaji had half a mind to leap in front of the nautch girl and intercept it, (a la Eknath Solkar) but his reflexes didn't cooperate. So, Balaji became a bitter, wise man (and perhaps with a vicarious satisfaction of seeing his money reach a deserving nautch girl).

As I write this, Tekedar must be tossing gold coins up there at all those dancing heavenly nymphs like Urvasi and Maneka, while fetching tea and आलू पराठे for Ved Vyas et al. Balaji should contemplate a tax write-off and bring the matter to a closure – or hope like hell that he has better luck in his next incarnation.

You know you're over fifty, if...

When a middle-aged woman in front of you addresses you as 'uncle' (before you could call her 'auntie'), and it no longer offends you.

17

A very special hooch

Learning from our Bollywood movies that if you want to be served good food you better be on the good side of the cook (I believe it was the actor Asrani in movie Rajni Gandha trying to impress Vidya Sinha by instructing the waiter to tell the cook who the order was for), we befriended the Nepali cook (I believe, his name was Ramesh) from our Hall I mess. It will be an understatement to say that during our stay in Hall I, especially during the summers, we were treated royally. After the mess closed (after 9:00 pm), he would often bring meat dishes, specially prepared for our taste, to our rooms and we would drink देशी शराब and chew on spicy chicken drumsticks or भुनां हुआ गोश्त often until the wee hours. There was no fear of missing our dinner because all we had to do was to let Ramesh know that there was a bottle of देशी सन्तरे की शराब waiting in our room.

One night after we did 'bottoms up' to a couple of bottles amongst four of us, Ramesh, feeling a little tipsy and thankful to our generosity, said, "साहिब बहुत दिनो से आप लोग हमको पिला रहें हैं, कभी हमारे गांव की भी शराब पीजिये."

"हां जरूर जरूर. क्या तुम्हारे गांव में भी शराब की दुकान है?" we asked.

"नहीं साहिब, हमारे गांव में शराब की दुकान कहां. हम लोग अपनी शराब खुद ही बनाते हैं," said Ramesh.

"तो लेके आओ. एक दिन तुम्हारी शराब की पार्टी करते हैं," we said.

"लेकिन साहिब उसमें कुछ पैसा लगेगा," he said.

"कोई बात नहीं. कितना पैसा लगेगा?" we asked.

"साहिब, एक बोतल का बीस रुपया लेते हैं," he said.

"बीस रुपया! ये तो सन्तरे की शराब से भी ज्यादा है," we said.

"अरे साहिब, हमारे गांव की शराब की सन्तरे की शराब से comprejen मत करिये," he said proudly.

"तब तो तुम्हारे गांव की शराब पीनी ही पड़ेगी," said one of us, handing him over two ten rupee bills.

The next day when we arrived at the mess at our usual time of 8:55 pm, Ramesh approached us and whispered into our ears, "साहिब, थोड़ी सी जगह रखियेगा. मैं कुछ ले कर आया हूं."

Hearing this, we immediately left our dinner and proceeded to our room anticipating to be surprised by some spicy meat dishes and the special hooch.

After a few minutes past nine, Ramesh arrived with a bottle of the 'special drink' and a bagful of food. It was a clear glass bottle showing the color of the drink. Although none of us had ever seen cow's urine in a clear glass bottle, but we knew that if we ever collected it in a bottle it will look very similar to what Ramesh had just brought. One of us took the bottle from him, unscrewed it and smelled it. He couldn't describe the smell, but from the twitching motion of his nostrils it was clear to the rest of us that the smell was nothing like he had ever experienced before. "Since it was a special drink, its smell couldn't be ordinary," we thought.

With a lot of anticipation and excitement, we all sat down as Ramesh served अन्डे की भुजिया और भुना हुआ गोश्त and poured us the drink.

Due to the hype created by Ramesh about the drink, we drank imagining how each drop must have been painstakingly distilled by the villagers. We took our time finishing the bottle. After we polished off the

bottle, we wanted some more as we were still waiting for the hooch to take control of our brain cells.

"साहिब मेरे पास एक बोतल और है. कया वो भी लाऊं?" asked Ramesh.

"अरे जाओ, तुरन्त ले कर लाओ," we told him.

He looked at us giving us a sly smile and gently rubbing his middle finger on his thumb (a signal for money). We all reached our pockets and emptied everything we had, which was a little less than 20 rupees.

"कोई बात नहीं साहिब, बाकी बाद में दे दीजियेगा," he said, promptly pockcting whatever we had collected.

Within a few minutes, Ramesh returned with another bottle of the same stuff.

We devoured the second bottle also in the next half an hour.

We waited, waited, and waited but there was no kick, no high, nothing.

"अरे रमेश ये कैसी शराब है? दो बोतल पी चुके हैं लेकिन अभी तक कुछ असर नहीं हुआ," we told him.

He took a deep breath, looked at us strangely, and spoke, "अरे साहिब, यही तो खास बात है इस शराब की. इस शराब का नशा बड़ा अजीब है; एक्चूली ये शराब आपको नशा देती है लेकिन पीने वाले को लगता है कि वो नशे मे नहीं है."

We looked at each other wondering, "Is that how cow's urine tastes like?"

When I was informed about this great initiative taken by our friend MA from Kolkata, those five beautiful years went wildly through my mind in a random but nostalgic way. I was enthused about putting down some of the experiences on a piece of paper but couldn't find time for it until just now at 2 am on a Sunday evening, or should I say Monday morning? Ragging used to be prevalent those days and though there was no physical torture per say, there used to be a lot of 'fear' of getting caught by a senior and taken to IIT Simla in his room to be presented to the hungry wolves waiting desperately for their prey! I was seen off by my parents at the railway station and they had told the TTC to wake me up when Kanpur came. And true to his promise, the TTC shook me up a few minutes before Kanpur and told me to pack up my 'hold-all' and move to the door which was the practice those days. I got down at the station and did the best thing that I could at that point of time – I found the nearest bench, put the suitcase under my head and the 'hold-all' under my legs and went off to sleep! When I was woken up again by the shouts of 'chay chay' at about 7.30 am, I realized that a new journey for me had just begun. I took a rickshaw to 'Bada chauraha' in search for a tempo which was supposed to take me to IIT campus, as per the instructions received from the institute. Excited about my first day at IIT, I got into an IIT bound tempo only to find that amongst several passengers on the tempo I was the only 'fresher'.

God! That was it and my new journey began right from that moment. I was ragged throughout the rough ride via Rawatpur and Kalyanpur to IIT campus and thereafter. The next few days were tough but also interesting in many ways as one was making new friends every day. Ragging went on unabated and after the first few days, one was tired and needed to catch up on sleep. I remember one of our friends, SD had brought his brother along, and so we told the big brother to lock the five of us in one room on the second floor. That was cool. He obliged and left for my room in another wing. In the middle of the night we felt the pressure in our bladders building up! The room was locked from outside and unfortunately there were no mobile phones or BBM services those days and there was no way we could communicate with the outside world. The big brother was presumably fast asleep in my room. After some time the urge became unbearable and all five of us were in a bad shape! Suddenly someone suggested "let's pee out of the window" and wow what a boon of a suggestion, we thought. And then someone else suggested why don't we all do it together and have a competition to see who finishes the last and who aims the farthest. That was a great feeling, as we eased ourselves, and a

great competition too in the early hours of the day. I was the runner up but can't recall now who the winner was; maybe it was our friend MA from Kolkata! The next day we played it safe and spent the night at Kalyanpur railway station! No one could really sleep that night but sure there were no bladders bursting and no villains looking for clueless 'freshers'.

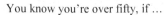

You know you're over fifty, if ...

Your grandchildren ask you, 'Grandpa, did you own a pet dianosaur when you were a kid?'

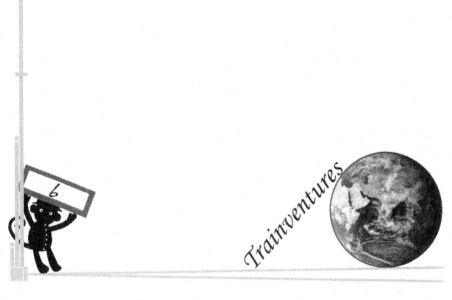

Going home to deep South was such a fascinating adventure that it still ranks among the bravest things I have ever done in my life. Since the mid-sem holidays were too brief for a trip home, we Southies had to wait an entire semester before we could set sail. I would have severe craving for home, amma's food, the cute thing next doors etc. etc. – so much so, I would even start feeling guilty about lying to dad about my grades.

When we were younger and more foolish, the entire Southy gang would hang around a non-descript desk in the administrative office to get 'concession forms' and faithfully go to the Kanpur Central railway station to be the millionth persons in the queue in front of a i-pad sized reservations counter. Occasionally we would get lucky and be rewarded with a reservation. We would then somehow extricate ourselves from the milling crowds, head straight toward Chung Fa and treat ourselves to some goo-ey mess and get back to the hostel just in time to formally start that long end-semester 'mugging session'. Over the years, of course, it became 'cool' to travel unreserved. And it became 'cooler' to be a फथरू. Yes, only the मग्घूs reserved train tickets.

Exams done, I would head straight to the barber for a long overdue haircut (under strict orders from dad) and a well deserved चम्पी. Then it would be time to ferret out all the old newspapers and assignment sheets and sell them to the रद्दीवाला. Never mind that the 'market price' of रद्दी

would come down drastically the last couple of days of the semester. I needed money – any money – to see me through my long train ride. Packing was as simple as shoving a scoop of dirty clothes into a borrowed, sorry-looking bag. That done, it was time to bid a tearful farewell to Pancham, Ganga Ram and the Dry-clean बुढ्ढा and get out of the campus as one of those five guys clinging on to an already-packed tempo in a wildly exhilarating ride to the station. Goodbye IIT Kalyanpur!

We Southies had to catch a rickety old passenger train up to Jhansi, where we would intercept the south-bound train. We would pass through tiny villages named Orai, Ait, Kalpi and finally, in the dead of night, arrive at Jhansi junction. On really feisty trips, we did foray into downtown Jhansi and imbibed the local brew. But mostly, we would just wait and wait for the South-bound trains coming from Delhi.

And then it would happen. A tiny pin-head of a light would appear in the distant horizon.

"गाड़ी आ रही है," someone would say.

Suddenly the platform would transform into a battlefield, with चाय वालाs arming themselves with their trays and a million people suddenly popping up from nowhere. The situation would look very hopeless. But then, we had the IIT brains, right? So, we would have already haggled with some slimy looking coolies to push us (and our pitiful luggage) into the train – any compartment – for ten rupees.

The train would shiver, shudder and slump by the platform and then the biggest mass transfer would occur in and out of the train. झांसी की रानी might have fought the British valiantly. But let her try getting into the Madras-bound Grand Trunk express.

Since we used to be reasonably thin and slithery, our plan would work. We would be already in the bowels of the compartment in the first push into the train. We would see the poor porter some twenty five light years away. Our fee, the ten rupees, would pass at least fifteen hands and ultimately reach him somehow. Fifteen minutes later, we had already called the train conductor 'uncle' and finagled a berth out of him. (He would have 'given berth to us', if you don't mind a bit of old fart humor)

Twenty minutes later, we would be reunited with our luggage and scarcely a half an hour later, we would be blissfully asleep.'

After going across seven seas and seven mountains – and traversing through the state of Andhra Pradesh for one whole day, the train would finally stagger into the Madras Central station, where धोतीs fly at half-mast and flies fly full blast. And only T. R. Ramdas would be left to continue on to Trivandrum.

Remember the sixth semester? It was strike-shortened and IITK closed early, sine die or something – pardon my Latin – and we all had to return to the campus a tad early, to write our postponed end-sem exams?

K. S. Balaji and I were returning from Chandigarh. And for a change, we even reserved our seats in the Kalka mail. When the train huffed and puffed into the station, we discovered our ticket reservations were only a suggestion and already twenty burly people were sitting where we were supposed to be sitting. After a bit of an argument and much pleading, they yielded a little and we had just enough space to park half an ass on the plank.

Then a spectacle happened. A shriveled old lady, crammed into a चूड़ीदार कमीज़ stood up and told us that she was allotted the upper berth – it was a two tier compartment – and since she was old and frail and could not climb up on to the berth, how about you guys - all twenty of you - go upstairs and sit there while she slept on the plank downstairs?

The twenty burly guys and we laughed. Nobody bought her deal. Next, her daughter argued her case and still there were no takers. Having given up, the old lady tried to climb on to the berth on her own. She raised her hands and grabbed the berth and kept moving her legs up and down, hoping that some magical force would propel her upstairs. It was so hilarious that I was laughing uncontrollably, whereupon her daughter turned toward me and uttered these golden words.

"हंसते हो क्यों बेटे? तुम भी एक दिन बुढ्ढे होगे।"

27

Call it a curse; call it a prophecy, but her words have come true and I have now become a terminal बुढ्ढा, approaching the last station of my life. These days I am mortally scared of walking on streets where little kids play फट्टा

cricket, for fear of being hit by their cover drives, and hurting what once used to be fondly referred to as the family jewel. Nubile young girls, when standing in front of me, no longer feel threatened by me and look at me as a benign uncle. Whereas I once used to cross check others' CPIs and SPIs, now I compare others' blood pressure numbers and sugar levels. And yes, I book lower berths or middle berths – very close to the bathroom - when I travel.

Well, on to my story.

Then the incredible happened. Balaji did the chivalrous. He stood up and stuck one of his legs on the seat. The old woman now had a sort of a step ladder to help her climb up. A couple of the burly guys led the cheers and helped too and she was gingerly hoisted upstairs to her rightful berth.

Everyone happy, end of the story – No, wrong.

Barely fifteen minutes after she had climbed on to her berth, she had to come down to do choo choo. She never bothered to climb back up again to her berth. And so, she sat with the rest of the twenty of us on the wooden plank. (Can't remember if she joined in the तीन पत्ती with the rest of the crowd) What else? At Subzi Mandi or some place fifteen more burly guys entered and sat on the upper berth anyway.

Moral of the story – There is no such thing as a thin Punjabi, Sunil Satija excepting.

You know you're over fifty, if...

You nominate Homer Simpson for a character actor award.

29

India was undergoing a political turmoil. The common man was disgusted with perceived government apathy towards widespread graft. The job market looked bleak. Under this backdrop, IITK atmosphere presented a strange, colorful and exciting ambience located somewhere between Vyasa and Wilde, Wodehouse and Vauldeville. For some, the campus was a sort of lunatic asylum and meant to keep young men out of mischief. For the balance, it was time to focus on their CV improvement – some working hard to lift their CPI, some working on competitive exams and the rest for migration to US in search for Gold. **Jh** was not the one who wanted to be part of this rat race and believed that everything which needs to be known can only be learnt after you are out of IIT. He was thinking hard on other options. One fine morning he woke up with a bright idea. "How about fighting an election to become a Senator." This, he thought, would be a good top-up on his CV for opportunities in the changing political landscape of India. His mind wandered to find a way for implementation of this idea. Not able to find any solution and unable to keep his misplaced excitement to himself, he entered **Mo**'s room, just a few doors down his own room.

"अरे यार, एक समस्या है," he said.

Mo listened patiently but was surprised as to how **Jh** could come out with such an out-of-box idea – he has no past political experience nor has a mass following nor has the personality to influence the voters.

"अबे दिमाग तो ठीक है?" **Mo** asked, peering through his glasses.

Ignoring the question and to impress upon his political acumen, **Jh** said in a calm voice "अरे यार अपने batch का political landscape समझो. इसके चार parts हैं – SS gang, T gang, commies & the 'परवाह नहीं' gang. आखिरी वाले में 40% हैं, इसको पकड़ना है."

Slowly the idea was sinking into **Mo**'s head. He asked, "मगर कैसे?"

Pat came the reply from **Jh** "तुम्हारा तो इनके साथ काफी उठना-बैठना है. इनको किसी तरह से लपेटो and tell them that politics is too serious a matter to be left to the politicians. तुम तो उस्ताद हो, तुम्हारे तो बायें हाथ का खेल है."

To ward off this challenge tossed at him, **Mo** put up a brave front and said "इसके लिये २०० रुपये का खर्चा है." For **Jh** this was a big jolt and without saying a word he walked out of the room. With a sigh of relief **Mo** started his morning chores.

Then three day after **Mo** saw **Jh** waiting for him in his room with 200 bucks in his hand. Whether this was a sign of desperation or an act of divine force having told **Jh** to put his full trust in **Mo** for the job, is still to be answered. Confused and left with no options, **Mo** took the possession of the bills...........

Ra was taken in confidence and a strategy was hatched. "The only reason we should be part of this election is to find out if the polls selected the right candidates" was the underline theme on which the strategy rested.

Feelers were sent with a rider that if **Jh** wins there would be a gala party invitation and the invitation is subject to your proxy vote to **Jh**. The response was overwhelming as many thought that one's duty as a voter should not interfere with one's pleasure in the slightest degree. The word soon spread. One of the candidates, VN from SS gang, felt threatened. His gang reacted with posters all over Hall 1 demanding to make **Jh**'s candidature null & void for adopting unconstitutional means to win the elections.

"The golden rule of practical politics is to ignore the facts. This free negative publicity improves your chances", **Mo** lectured visibly disturbed **Jh.** A dark horse was in the making and we felt it would be prudent to ignore this attack.

Jh was overjoyed as he won his seat with maximum first preference votes creating history. Luckily, VN also won. The party started and celebrations continued till late night with some gulping more pegs than their body could support. What incited them is not known but the next day they were called by the warden for questioning their unruly behavior and broken window panes in some of the bathrooms. They were let off with a minor punishment and some fine.

After few days, in the middle of a bull session, **Jh** raised a question.

"मैं left से align करूं या right से? दोनों तरफ से pressure है." This was a

true senator speaking. An ideological debate started and as usual, with divided opinion. Then somebody instructed **Jh**, "Go to the washroom and pee with your family jewels freely hanging. See the direction of your projectile. That should answer your question". After sometime **Jh** returned, smiled wickedly, and announced "ना left में था, ना right में था, middle में था".

However, doubts were expressed by someone regarding hands-free piddling without any slightest L or R tilt, because almost everyone had experienced some tilt. Doubts were also expressed about accuracy of measurement of the angle of the pee-projectile while urinating in a toilet, be it of Indian or Western design. So, it was decided that **Jh** would piddle hands-free in an open plain ground and tilt towards L or R, if any, would be measured with maximum accuracy within a tolerance of ± 5° angle. For this test, Tennis Court behind Hall I was chosen as an appropriate place, as it had plain surface with perpendicular lines already painted on it and also it had a partially blocked view from general public so that **Jh** could concentrate on urinating rather than worry about being watched. **Jh** consented for it and performed his hands-free piddle under the watchful eyes of **Mo**. Surprisingly; the piddle landed on the perpendicular line only, without any L or R deviation and **Jh**'s claim was thus vetted. It was therefore decided that **Jh** would take neutral/centralist stands in all his senatorial activities. **Jh** strictly followed it.

Till this date **Jh** is a centrist but still looks both ways before crossing a one-way street.

 You know you're over fifty, if...

The sum of your diastolic blood pressure, HDL, triglycerides, your wife's waistline, your waistline and the number of days since you last had sex rapidly approaches the Bombay stock exchange SENSEX Index.

We came, we waited, we left

Circa 1972, first semester....and we have a whole bunch of young first year students, fresh faced out of school, and reveling in their new found freedom, particularly not to 'dress' for college/class.

The story takes off in L7, where everyone is waiting for Prof. CNR Rao to arrive, to take a Chm 101 lecture. Mr. Anupam Kappor (aka Gaf) was dressed in his sartorial best, comprising of a pair of shorts (half pants) of a particularly ugly lemon yellow color. Somebody early on had commented upon the color as reminding him of his morning visit to the bogs.

Anyway the class is getting restless, since Prof. Rao had not yet arrived, even after ten minutes or so, and there were loud whispers about the best way to exit. As was the norm, everyone was waiting for someone else to take the initiative.

Soon Mr. Gaf takes the initiative, and saunters down the L7 aisle to the blackboard in his eye catching yellow shorts, and proceeds to write on the black board 'We came, We waited, We Left.' Of course there was a huge roar in the auditorium as people took it as the signal to bunk. However, as Annu was walking out, we/he noticed Prof. M.V. George running after him, shouting 'come back.' Nobody had noticed MVG's

presence in L7, as he had been sitting in a corner at the rear of the lecture hall. Annu of course had the shock of his life, and sprinted out of L7. While the rest of us who were contemplating a snooze back in the room, froze to silence. Prof. George was seen shaking his fist at the fast disappearing yellow apparition, and muttering that he will teach a lesson (not Chm 101) to 'that pantless Kapuuur' (my attempt at MVG's strong Malayalee accent).

You know you're over fifty, if...

Your loud farts in public embarrass you – because they are not loud enough.

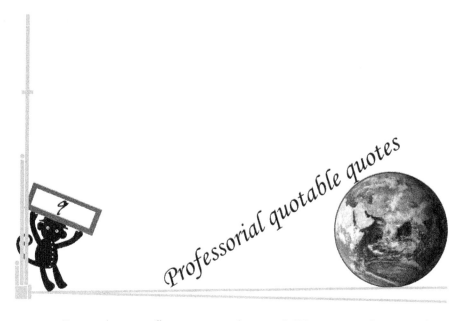

Professorial quotable quotes

Remember our first semester lectures? We were so impressed by so many faculty members that my memories are still fresh. All those exciting lectures by CNR Rao, tethered to the microphone cable, with the mike Surd assiduously setting the volume and CNR's inimitable 'Am I audible in the rear?' Actually not so inimitable, because Mukesh Anjaria enthralled all of us on numerous occasions with his CNR Rao impersonations – as well as 'Obb-rai'. And Prof. Mohanty's Signature 'You gib me epsilon and I bill gib you delta'.

And this happened in our first semester. Prof. Waghmare was our physics tutor and we were suitably impressed by him with all the hype about a so-called 'Waghmare Potential' that allegedly made him quite famous in the scientific circles. When we asked him about what it was, he would go 'तुम सीखोगे'. Anyways, toward the end of the first semester, the mess workers were on strike and on one of those high voltage days, when volunteers had to step in and cook our food in the mess, Prof. Waghmare turned to the class and asked – and mind you, these were the pre-politically correct days – 'Poonam (Mathur), कुकिंग आती है?' I can't remember what her answer was. In an unrelated career move, I think Prof. Waghmare left IIT K soon after. I went on to do a Ph.D. in Physics and I never encountered any Waghmare Potential. I guess Waghmare Potential is yet another potential whose true potential is never realized.

How about Prof. Shetty squatting on the L7 dais with his pet Tablas, refusing to get up and demanding in his New York/Konkan drawl 'कोई गाना गायेगा तो हम तबला बजायेगा...'

This is a classic, allegedly from a Metallurgy faculty member. Since no Met student from our batch attended any classes, I am unable to confirm this incident. The fac. Member apparently was spinning a yarn about his good old Yank days, "The Americans are confused by India. I had to tell them, John, remember axiom – 'All Sikhs Singhs. But all Singhs not Sikhs'."

This is private one. Quite a few people and I were waiting outside a physics faculty member's office – me to get 'hadkao'ed for something or the other and the rest of them on usual business. There was even a lady waiting for him, but had to leave without meeting him. When the faculty member finally arrived, I went in and told about a lady waiting for him and he went "That's not a lady. That's Fatima..."

Prof. Singh and I were united by fate. Both of us were big fatrus and both of us were in the Five Year Integrated M. Sc. Physics program. There was a despicable 16 weightage lab course in our fourth year and both of us had zero aptitude to do any of those classic experiments meant to help self-discover amazing scientific facts. Instead, the only discovery we made was that there was a 'dark room' lab, where, if we so chose, we could do optical experiments. Prof. Singh and I would hide in that Lab for three hours and chitchat about all kinds of things in total darkness – mostly politics, when one day, suddenly there was light in the dark room and in barged a very loudly barking physics faculty member (who shall not be named). I have never seen Prof. Singh being that quiet and defensive, started to stammer "I mean….". when the faculty member continued to bark "What do you mean I mean, My meaning is quite clear…."

Oh, well. Those were indeed the days.

You know you're over fifty, when…

You find during the class reunions that the old flames you used to have crush on look even older.

धीना चाल, a family game

This is a short episode that needs to be shared as a public service to the group considering that most of us are now in the state of life when our children are grown up and we have plenty of free time at hand, but we don't have enough energy to play the long marathon tennis and badminton matches. धीना चाल, an interesting game that I learned during my trekking trip to Nepal with two of our batch mates may be worth learning. This is an ideal game to pass time with friends. You can even play this with your spouse.

Three of us trekked for about eight hours from Pokhra (the second largest city of Nepal) to reach a picturesque small hamlet (I forget the name). The view was just breathtaking. You could see the magnificent snow-covered peaks as far in the yonder as you could see. Exhausted and thirsty, we were looking for some tea shop to fight the bone-chilling cold. Spotting a streak of smoke coming out of a little hut at a distance uphill, we mustered whatever strength we had left and trudged towards it. As hoped, it was a little tea shop. We greeted the old man who was stoking the fire in a make-shift oven and boiling tea in an aluminum kettle. We unloaded our rucksacks and made ourselves comfortable on a raised rock platform near the fire.

"चाय मिलेगी?" we asked.

"हां शाब, जरूर मिलेगी," grinned the old man, revealing his two missing front teeth.

"और खाने के लिये क्या है?" we asked.

"शाब, खाने के लिये बिशकुट हैं," he said.

We drank our tea and munched on the biscuits while absorbing the heat from the fire. As we were enjoying our tea we noticed two middle-aged men sitting almost motionless face-to-face across another rock platform intently staring at the middle of the platform. First we didn't pay much attention to them but our curiosity peaked to see them not move for about ten minutes straight continuing to stare at the middle of the platform.

"ये लोग क्या कर रहे हैं?" we asked the old man.

"ये लोग धीना चाल खेल रहे हैं शाब," he replied, "बहुत अच्छा गेम है शाब. आप भी देखिये जाकर."

Believing it to be a local board game, we walked to the two men, holding our tea cups, to observe the game. The men casually glanced at us and went back to staring at the table (the rock platform). There was no checker board or any sketched pattern on the table. There were two quarters (चवन्नी) on the table, one each in front of the men. From the intensity by which they were staring at the table, we didn't feel like disturbing them. We stood there quietly and tried to understand how this game was being played. After about ten minutes of total concentration, one of the men picked up the other guy's चवन्नी and put it in his pocket. The guy who lost the चवन्नी was obviously unhappy, but like a good sportsman he took another चवन्नी out of his pocket and replaced it with the one he just lost. Then they went back to their staring routine again.

We couldn't contain ourselves. "ये तुम लोग क्या खेल रहे हो?" we asked.

"धीना चाल खेल रहे हैं शाब. आप खेलियेगा?" said one of the men.

Before we tried our luck with this game we needed to know the rules of the game. From the postures of these two men and the intensity with which they were absorbed in the game, it was clear that the game required some fierce mental concentration, which we all believed we had plenty of. "ये कैसे खेलते हैं?" we asked.

"बहुत शिम्पिल है शाब. Players अपने अपने शामने एक एक शिक्का (coin) रखते हैं," he began to explain, "जिशके भी शिक्के पर मक्खी (a fly) पहले बैठेगी वो जीत जायेगा."

We looked at each other in amazement with our mouths open wide. "Wow! What a creative game!" we thought. Now we understood why these guys were sitting motionless during the game – to lure flies to their coin.

"आप खेलियेगा?" he asked.

"Why not?" I volunteered while the others cheered.

After losing five चवन्नीs, I had an idea to turn the game in my favor and show these locals the prowess of IIT brain. Before taking the next चवन्नी out of my pocket I casually put my pointer finger deep inside my nostrils to wet it with 'fly-nector'. As I took out the next coin, I stealthly smeared my nostril fluid on the coin. While the other two IITians didn't notice anything unusual, this act did not escape the eagle eyes of one of the local men.

"शाब, ये शिक्का आप नहीं यूज़ कर शकते हैं," said the man.

"Why?" I asked, acting surprised.

"शाब, वो शिक्का गन्दा हो गया है. उशपे तो मक्खी पहले बैठेगी ही," he said.

41

"Oh," I replied, pretending innocence and trying to hide my embarrassement of being caught cheating.

He made me wash my hands and the coin before proceeding.

To cut the long story short, we lost about eight चवन्नीs. Before we realized we had been playing धीना चाल for more than three hours. Moreover, after the game we all felt very relaxed and invigorated ready to begin our next trek.

We would strongly recommend this game if you want to have some quality time with your loved ones. It may even be worthwhile to have a धीना चाल tournament during our reunion.

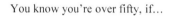

You know you're over fifty, if...

You know what PSA stands for. (For the younger ones, the PSA is Prostate Specific Antigen)

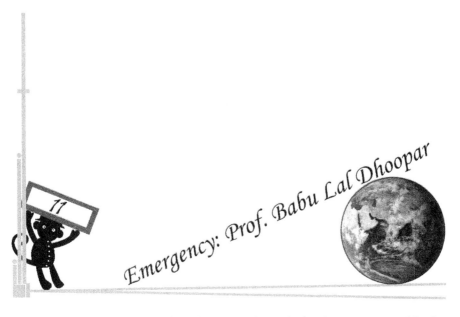

Emergency: Prof. Babu Lal Dhoopar

We are the generation that went through the Emergency and had a ring side view of it. We were affected and yet not affected. We were affected when our beloved Prof. B.L. Dhoopar was arrested for RSS links. What a shock that was! What danger did he pose to the security of the nation? Was he doing anything clandestine?

He was a towering personality, and the true Jat. "ढाई किलो का हाथ" hadn't been invented then, but he would have weighed in at Three kilos definitely! And inspite of taking लाठी drills in Khakhi shorts, he was a very mild person, who would not hurt a fly. And he was whisked away to unknown destination for over six months. No one knew whether he was alive or he had been eliminated as 'enemy of the State' because at that time, 'Indira was India' and 'India was Indira', so any one who did not like Indira had to be taken care of.

Having tasted full freedom in the first three years, we were also not fond of the Emergency and restrictions imposed. For a while people thought it was good, but Prof. Dhoopar's arrest angered everyone.

After about six months, word suddenly spread in the campus that Professor साहब was coming back. No one was spreading the word, but it was all over the campus, instantly and there was no SMS in those days. The institute authorities probably did not want to arrange a welcome,

43

because the Emergency was still on. Without anyone saying it or announcing it, everyone knew by which train he would arrive... and though there was no official arrangement to go to the station, everyone wanted to be there to receive Professor साहब and definitely all Mechanical guys.

There was a mad rush of students headed for the station, and the road to station from Parade stop was full of IITK guys, walking, in ricks.

The platform was chock a block with students and the notoriously hungry crowd had not bothered about lunch or anything; they crowded the platform from noon. There were slogans mainly of Prof. Dhoopar जिन्दाबाद, IITK जिन्दाबाद, or whatever. By then another slogan had become popular.. "ना नर है ना नारी है ये तो Narain Dutt Tiwari है," but I don't know if that slogan was shouted. Of course everyone knew that too much of ruckus could invite police action, so apart from a general buzz, no heavy activities were indulged in. His 'शाखा' members were waiting with garlands.

Finally after a long wait, the train arrived. There was total silence all around, even though there were a couple of thousand students there. And then, as the train came to a halt, and Professors साहब was sighted at the door, there was a sudden crescendo, just a collective sigh of relief, and then Prof. Dhoopar अमर रहो, जिन्दाबाद, and what have you. The noise was like the heavens bursting. There were many tears, and many guys went hysterical, there was total sense of elation, that our warrior had come back home. It was not about politics, but the fact that politics and academics don't mix, no one could turn the event into his advantage - it was 2000 student's individual homage and respect for a great teacher.

Of course he was carried on our shoulders to the exit, but everyone noticed that this mountain of a man known for his erectness in body and spirit had been badly treated and was not really able to walk properly. And in that instant, seeds of Indira Gandhi's defeat in the next election were sown. I mean preventive detention, holding incommunicado were alright, but what right did the scum policemen, who even today in UP are not fit to clean toilets, have to physically abuse him.

And that was what the IIT spirit revealed to me that day. If the issue is right, no one needs any cajoling, and everyone can be expected to

do the right thing. Respect where respect is due is given unconditionally, in whole measure and without hesitation.

I had no idea of Prof. Dhoopar's status or his role in the RSS, ok he was a big shot. But 25 years later, I was traveling in a train which L.K. Advani had boarded. And I took the chance to meet him and greet him between stations, even though I had to get past commandoes and stuff, but while train was moving, the security was relaxed. I met with Advaniji, and spoke to him for a while. Then told him that my respect for the Sangh came from a teacher in Kanpur! And by God, he immediately asked, "Who, Dhoopar साहब?" He is great and a respected man. It was then that I realised Prof. Dhoopar's real humility.

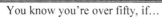

You know you're over fifty, if...

You don't worry about secrets because your friends don't remember them either.

Make-up का make-up

Jh was a lover of nature. He believed that it takes 15 trees to produce the amount of paper that we use to write one exam. This belief was always in conflict with his compulsion of writing exams. The exam system of this five-year-program at IIT was getting on his nerves. By the time he reached his final year, he had mastered the art of dodging exams with a changed belief that the performance based grading system is for confusing a young mind methodically.

IIT has a unique exam system which is based on long-rope strategy. If a student is unintentionally or intentionally avoiding an exam, the faculty is under instruction not to leave him instead give him a make-up exam. This was to ensure that you kick them out of the institute as soon as possible. Make-up exams were generally mellowed down version of the main exam and relative grading was not a factor.

Jh had missed one of end semester exam and his request for a make-up exam was accepted and had to be given within 10 days. The D-day approached and Jh was not mentally ready for the test. Jh approached the Professor.

"Sir, I am not ready for the exam," Jh said with a sad tone.

"Why, what happened?" asked the Professor (P).

"I......," he hesitated and continued, " I had to go home; one of my close relative was not keeping well and I had to take care of him."

"Ohhh.........how is he now?" asked **P**.

"Better. Now I can concentrate on studies. Please give me 7 days more," said **Jh.**

"OK. But this is your last chance. If you again bunk, I will be left with no option but to give you an F," said **P** firmly.

"Thank you, Sir. I will not fail my words this time," said **Jh** in an assuring tone.

For **Jh** all days were same and dates had seized to be of any interest to him. He had been taken over by the lazy ambience of the campus. His true token of greatness was his ability to forget, specially the exams.

It was a summer afternoon; **Mo** was relaxing in his room contemplating how to clear his summer course. Suddenly his thoughts were disturbed by a nervous **Jh** standing in front of him.

"क्या हुआ?" asked **Mo.**

"गोली हो गयी. डेढ़ बजे से make-up था, भूल गये. अभी ढायी बज रहे हैं," said **Jh** with a shiver.

"अरे ....," said **Mo.**

"जल्दी से ambulance बुलाओ. कहो कि मेरे पेट में बहुत दर्द हो रहा है," said **Jh** putting his hand on **Mo**'s shoulder.

In this world you have three kinds of friends: the friends who love you, the friends who do not trouble their heads about you, and the friends who hate you. For **Mo**, he did not fall in any of the above categories and was a friend because of his well-dressed foolish ideas. One of **Jh**'s ideas of a play with a punch of suspense, thrill & romance titled 'गां...में उंगली किसने की?' had left a lasting impression on **Mo**. To reinforce the friendship bond, **Mo** staged this play in the fresher's night with the help of freshers to convey his friendship towards **Jh**.

47

'क्योंकी हर friend जरूरी होता है' - **Mo** sprang-up in action and the ambulance arrived.

Jh was taken very carefully to the ambulance which proceeded straight towards Dr. **L** residence. It was 3.30 pm of peak summer time and generally for doctors it was the time to relax at home. As soon as **Jh** saw Dr. **L** coming out of his house, his acting skills were at its peak.

"हाय मर गया. मोहन जरा पेट सहला दो. अजीब लग रहा है," **Jh** said, caressing his stomach. **Mo** did as instructed.

"What is the problem?" asked Dr. **L,** admiring the coordinated acting skills of **Jh** and **Mo.**

Without waiting for an answer, Dr. **L** instructed the ambulance attendant "इनको hospital ले जाओ और glucose चढ़ाओ."

Jh was laid to rest on one of the beds in the Health Center with Glucose Drip. **Mo** was by his side giving him moral support.

"Professor को अब बता दो कि हम दीर शन्का से परेशान हैं और nurse लोगों नें मुझे glucose drip से बांध दिया है," **Jh** said to **Mo.**

An application was written and **Mo** carried it to the professor.

"Sir, **Jh** is in the hospital and has given this letter," **Mo** said, handing over the letter to the Professor.

The professor read the letter and said with an irritating look on his face, "Now I have the most perfect confidence in his indiscretion. Ask him to meet me once he is out of this mess."

It was now 7.30 pm and Dr. **L** was on his regular hospital round. His first patient was **Jh.** He looked at him, his expressions similar to a butcher having a look at the goat before slaughter. **Jh** did not react but looked straight in his eyes.

"Sister.........! Take out the drip before dinner. Give another drip tomorrow..... after lunch. और Dinner में boiled vegetables and खिचड़ी, both बिना नमक के," said Dr. **L** and moved to the next patient. **Jh** looked at the nurse; she smiled and his heart skipped a beat.

Jh was cursing God as to how he can set definite limits on man's wisdom, but set no limits on his stupidity – and that's not fair! Shrugging off these thoughts he pacified himself by saying that the only good in pretending is the fun we get out of fooling ourselves that we fool somebody. Suddenly his thoughts were broken by sweet female voice.............he looked up.

"आपका drip निकालना है," the nurse said.

"हां हां जरूर. ये catheter भी निकाल देना," said Jh.

"नहीं. कल आपको फिर से एक और drip देनी है," said the nurse.

"दूसरे हाथ में नया लगा दीजिये," said Jh casually.

The nurse obliged. "Thanks heaven! The sun has gone in, and I don't have to go out and enjoy it," said Jh, trying to hide his intentions.

Next day around 12.30 pm, Jh slipped out of the hospital and headed straight to the shopping center. His destination – Red Rose restaurant.

"एक मलाई कोफ्ता, एक पालक पनीर, और दो बटर नान... जल्दी से लाना. सालों ने भूखा मार दिया," **Jh** instructed the amused waiter.

As **Jh** was engrossed in admiring the मलाई कोफ्ता, he heard somebody speaking to him "Undoubtedly the desire for food has been, and still is, one of the main causes for indigestion". He looked up and it was the professor.

"Sir, apart from indigestion, I have 3 more maladies, but am otherwise very well," said **Jh** in a nervous tone.

"You mean to say that if a man stands with right foot on a hot stove and left foot in a freezer, statistically, on an average, he is comfortable," barked the professor.

"No Sir, I meant.....................I have just become OK," replied **Jh.**

"Now even a medical certificate cannot save you from an F. The questions will be so designed that you will be unable to solve any problem," said the professor and walked to the table where his wife was waiting for lunch.

Jh was overjoyed. No more hassles. Now the make-up का make-up का make-up exam has been officially cancelled. Tension free, he came straight to **Mo**'s room.

"तुम कहां हो? Hospital तुम्हे ढूंढ रहा है. तुमने relieving formalities पूरी नहीं की हैं," **Mo** said in a disturbed tone.

Fast forward......Formal relieving exercise from the Health Center was completed and, as expected, **Jh** was awarded an F.

'समय की दीमक' has not been able to bring any change in **Jh.** He is still a person who gets up on a Saturday morning and has nothing to do, and by bedtime has it only half done.

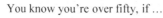

You know you're over fifty, if ...

Purchase prophylactic rubber in 12 packs – January, February, March,...

We were eagerly looking forward to our 4th year industrial tour. Majority of us going for the trip were from EE/ME Departments. A complete train coach was booked which would be our dwelling for the next 25 days. The route of our journey was carefully planned in consultation with the railways and industries we wished to visit. Just two days after our end Semester exams, we began our journey from Kanpur with our coach attached to a train going southwards.

There comes a time in every rightly-constructed guy's life when he has a raging desire to go somewhere and explore the forbidden territories. This was the time – for the serious ones, the hunting grounds were the factories and for the rest it was simply a फतरूगिरी escapade. After the overnight journey the train stopped at our first destination. The coach was detached from the train and parked in the station yard. Throughout the journey our chores were precisely tuned with the yard parking time. Sometimes on late running trains, we skipped our breakfast to avoid putting pressure on our nature's call. Luckily as a savior, this became a practice during the latter half of our tour, mainly to save money for better use.

Through many twist & turns our coach reached the last stop, Mumbai (then Bombay). By this time roughly 30% guys had reached a stage of managing themselves on borrowed cash. **Mo** was one of those who had exhausted his borrowing options but believed that with luck and resolution........the human mind can survive poverty. His mind wondered. The possibility of getting cash from his uncle residing in Andheri crossed his mind. **Ma**, **Bi**, and **Vi** were persuaded to finance the journey in return for a Dinner at **Mo**'s uncle place.

After purchasing tickets at VT station, the foursome boarded a train. They noticed a sweet looking girl in front of them engrossed in reading a book. Our animal instinct prodded us to lay bait and see if she would bite. One of us approached her and tried to strike a conversation, "How long will it take to reach Andheri," asked one of us. She responded and more questions followed. As this chit-chat continued towards the so called comfort zone - she rose suddenly, picked up her purse, gave a heart skipping good-bye smile, and marched off towards the exit gate. Moments later, as the train stopped on a platform, she got down, waving at us and hurriedly disappeared into the crowd. देखा ना हाय रे, सोचा ना हाय रे, रख दी निशाने पे जान. We jumped out and, like trained blood hounds, sniffed around for her scent. She was nowhere to be seen. Looking back sometimes I have a feeling that ordinarily we were insane, but we had lucid moments when we were merely stupid.

Wondering why things are largely absurd, futile, and transitory, we strolled on crowded street outside the train station. We noticed a group of people huddled around a table on one of the side streets. Curious to find out, we squeezed our heads into the openings between the onlookers. People were taking turns betting on a card game. It was quite a simple game. The dealer would place one card face up and the invite people to place a bet on whether the next card dealt would be of smaller of bigger value than the face-up card. Many people doubled their money right in front of our eyes. "It's simply a probability game," we thought. Though the probability theory was not the claim-to-fame for any of us, the game was simple enough that, we thought, we could outsmart the guy. The opened card was five of diamond. **Ma** put a bet of one rupee that the next dealt card would be higher value. The man shuffled the deck and opened the card – it was two of clubs. The dealer dealt another face up card. This time it was queen of spades. "There are only three cards higher than queen. This is a sure win," thought **Ma**. He bet ten rupees that the next card would be of lower value. The dealer shuffled the deck and the next card was Ace. "What the hell is going on?" we wondered. **Vi** told the dealer that he would bet additional money only if the deck is shuffled before we made the bet.

The dealer agreed. The next face up card was again queen. He bet ten rupees for the next card to be of smaller value. As the dealer was getting ready to shuffle the deck, **Vi** held his hand and reminded him of the agreement. The dealer put another card on the table. It was a five. As **Vi** looked at the dealer for his prize money, the dealer took his ten rupee bill and looked at others encouraging them to bet. "What about my winnings?" asked **Vi**. "Which winnings? You said the next card would be of higher value. You just lost," he said, with an obvious threat in his voice. "There are four of us. We can teach this goon a lesson," we thought.

"सीधी तरह हे हमारे पैसे निकालो, वरना हम दूसरा तरीका अपनाते हैं," said **Ma**, adding a little meanness to his voice.

As soon as he finished delivering the threat, we were surrounded by five of the dealer's mean looking henchmen.

"चुपचाप यहां से कट लो, वरना इतनी मार पड़ेगी कि पहचान मे नहीं आओगे," said one of the men as he took out a रामपुरी चाकू from his left pocket flashing its shining blade.

This was the ideal time to deliver the famous Raj Kumar's dialogue from the film Waqt, 'ये बच्चो के खेलने की चीज़ नहीं है. इसे रख लो वरना उँगली कट जायेगी', but outnumbered and outgunned (or outknived) we

retreated. However, **Ma** was not ready to throw in the towel yet. With the speed of light, he quickly devised a plan.

"ये लोग ऐसे नहीं मानेंगे. तुम यहीं रुको, मैं अभी अपने DSP Uncle को phone करके आता हूं," said **Ma**, making sure that the men heard the words 'DSP Uncle' clearly. **Mo, Bi,** and **Vi** wondered why **Ma** never told them about his DSP uncle posted in Mumbai.

The mention of DSP got the goons' attention. A couple of them followed **Ma** to a restaurant. **Ma** requested the manager if he could make a telephone call to the DSP's office, to which the manager promptly agreed.

The mannerism of the men following **Ma** was clearly changing.

"अरे साहब, पुलिस को बीच में क्यों डालते हैं," said one of the men as **Ma** dialed a phony number.

Seeing that his plan was working, **Ma** ignored the man's plea.

"क्या DSP श्रीखन्डे साहब हैं? उनसे बोलिये कि उनका भतीजा लाइन पर है," **Ma** spoke into the phone.

As **Ma** pretended to wait for the DSP to come on line, he felt a tap on his shoulder.

"ये लीजिये साहब अपने पैसे. अगर हमको पहले पता होता कि आप लोग पुलिस के आदमी है तो बात यहां तक नहीं बढ़ती," said the dealer handing us a total of 21 rupees, our total bet amount.

Acting to play tough, **Ma** said, "अरे नहीं नहीं. अब पैसे तो तुमसे हमारे DSP Uncle ही लेगें आकर."

"अरे साहब नराज मत होइये. ले लीजिये पांच रुपये और रखिये," said the dealer, slipping another five rupee bill.

Meanwhile **Mo, Bi,** and **Vi** walked into the restaurant. Seeing that the plan worked flawlessly and that it was time to drop the curtains, **Mo** added, "छोड़ो जाने दो. अपने DSP Uncle को अब मत बुलाओ."

Victorious and richer by five rupees, **Ma** pocketed the 26 rupees and all four of us walked out, each of us feeling six feet tall.

After spending some time in a Dhaba for a cup of tea, we boarded the next train to Andheri where the ticket checkers were looking for their ticketless murgas. Already late and with homemade dinner in our minds, we showed our tickets to the checker. It was a rude shock when we were ordered to stand in the line of ticketless travelers. We reacted, "टिकट तो है." The TC looked at us, his eyes gauging our worth – "चुप चाप खड़े रहो, अभी बताते हैं." It was past 9.00 pm, and we were wondering, "Uncle को कैसे झेलोगे अगर देर हो जायेगी?" After some time, it was our turn to be grilled.

TC asked, "कब टिकट कटाया है?"

We said in unison, "चार बजे."

Pat came another question, "अभी कितना बज रहा है?"

We had never faced such quizzing before - not even during our ragging sessions with seniors.

"क्या आप हम लोगों की घड़ी चेक कर रहें हैं?" we blurted showing our irritation.

Raising our tickets in his hand, he mentioned "ये टिकट सिर्फ चार घन्टे के लिये ही है."

When we shrugged our shoulders telling him that we didn't know about it, his reply was, "Ignorenc iz no excooz in laa. Fine देना पड़ेगा," he said.

"कितना?" we asked.

"20 रुपया हर एक को."

All of us took out our I-card demanding concession as railways had already given us 50% for this tour. "No concession on fines," he said firmly. Already, out-of-money, we did not look much different from truly normal beggars.

Seeing us struggling for money, he said, "अच्छा चालीस में सबका काम हो जायेगा."

As soon as the TC said this, a ray of hope crossed us and we stood still to make up our mind. Seemingly to overlook and read us with a smile - not telling what he read – he asked "कितने हैं?" **Mo** took out a 50 paisa coin proclaiming his net worth. Rest followed and the contributions summed up to Rs.2.25. Sensing being outwitted and further waste of time on us looking unproductive, he decided to take us to the railway court.

In one of the bull sessions, **Mo** had lectured on his fascination for crabs. He professed that more than any of the God's creatures, crabs have formulated the perfect philosophy of life. Elaborating, he had said "whenever a crab is confronted by a great moral crisis in life, he first makes up his mind what is right, and then move sideways as fast as it can." What a philosophy, and it got registered somewhere in our minds.

There was an immediate urge to run but looking around we could not figure out a suitable escape point except the exit gate of the platform where 2 TCs were casually checking tickets. The crabs decided - no more of stupidity - and followed the TC. Barely 10 yards from the official exit gate, our fears were just nearing the bursting point when suddenly two of us caught the TC's hand to stop him from going any further. The TC and the other 2 looked puzzled. Sometimes, courage is fear that has said its prayers.

"Boss, कहानी खतम करो. बहुत band बजा हुआ है," one of us said.

With so many L7 movies behind us, courtesy SFS, we were very well versed with the science of touch– the first step towards heart. One of the hands went gently over his shoulder. "क्या कर रहे हो – छोड़ो मुझे," he said, irritated. Simultaneously, the second hand went up his shoulder. Having come closer, **Mo** whispered in the TC's ear, "चलो पहले आपका माथा ठन्डा करते हैं, फिर बात करेंगे."

Before anybody could realize, we were just 2 yards from the exit gate, we noticed that the 2 TCs at the gate were looking curiously at us. Avoiding eye contact with them, our hands tightened their grip and we started conversing loudly, "आज शर्मा जी (TC's name) ठन्डी लस्सी होयेगी, बहुत दिन हो गयें हैं." By this time Sharmaji had slackened and gave an embarrassing smile to the other 2 TCs. Once out, the last remaining resistance of Sharmaji collapsed. He was now a friend.

During the chat we were having while sipping our लस्सी, Sharmaji told us that he was caught 22 times ticketless before he got into this job. Now he travels freely without any fear. It was late and we abandoned our visit to M's uncle's place and went back to our coach for an empty stomach sleep.

It is better to have loafed and lost than never to have loafed at all. It helps remembering ourselves.

You know you're over fifty, if…

You have a party and your neighbors do not complain because they don't even know it.

57

A dream job

It must have been after 3rd semester that I decided to do a part-time job offered through student's dean affairs office. I clearly remember my 3rd semester when both my CPI and SPI were at the lowest and there was no room for going down any further. They had to come up so I decided to add on to this with a part-time job as a part of punishing myself and take some burden off of my parents' shoulders.

My first job was in our central library where I was working in the inter-library loan department. In those days when there was no internet or a common database, I wonder even now how it used to work. We used to get requests from research scholars of the member institutes (all 5 IITs, IISc and Central Gov. labs like BARC etc.) for a particular paper or topic. This request would be given to me and my job was to look for papers through catalogues in our library, and if found, collect them from the racks and give it to despatch for a two weeks loan to the member institutes. This is where for the first time I had interactions with a first generation Xerox machine with plate light and granules.

After working in the Library for two semesters I got a chance to work for our dear Health Center, a red building close to the girls' hostel. There I met Dr. Borwankar (I hope I remember how to spell his name) famous from IITK oath that we took many times during our orientation (ragging) not to forget this at least in this life. He was the Chief Medical officer so in a sense I was working for him. My first assignment was at the reception making new medical files of out-patients who were mostly the staff of IIT including our professors but the story is not about library or hospital it is something else …

After working at the reception for a few weeks, Dr. Borwanker called me into his office. Clueless as to why he called me for, I knocked at his door.

"May I come in sir?" I asked.

"Yes, yes, please do come in, आओ बैठो," he said, pointing towards an empty chair across his desk.

"I'm really happy with your dedication to work," he said.

"Thank you, Sir," I said hoping that he would probably recommend a raise in my hourly wages.

He put his glasses on the table and leaned forward towards me and said, "I am doing a project और मैं चाहता हूं कि तुम उसमें मेरी मदद करो."

I looked at him curiously expecting him to continue talking and tell me about this project.

He continued, "ये बहुत ही sensitive project है और इससे पहले कि मैं कुछ बताऊं, you must give me an assurance of confidentiality."

"What could this project be," I wondered as my curiosity peaked, "I have to know more about this confidential project."

"Sir आप मुझ पर पूरा भरोसा कर सकते हैं," I told him, dying to know the project.

I'm quite proud of myself that I have kept my commitment of confidentiality for the last 34 years. My friends, it is only now that I am revealing only some portions of that experience.

Once assured of my commitment to secrecy, Dr. Borwankar continued, "This is a project called Fertility Survey of IIT Kanpur. Among other things, we want to know, through this project, different family planning methods practiced by IIT families."

He continued, "All you have to do is to go to people's houses and have them fill out a questionnaire. So are you interested in doing this?"

"Sir, इस Project का Purpose क्या है?"

"The purpose is to better plan health and child care facility in the campus," he said handing me the two pages of the questionnaire.

I started reading the questionnaire. The first page was standard - names of all family members with age, sex, date of birth, etc. But as I read the second page, my excitement meter climbed up rapidly. It had questions like - Did they have any miscarriage? When and how the children were born - Normal or C section? Did they have any complications? The most interesting was the question about their choice (actual question was what method they used) of family planning methods.

"Sir ये तो बहुत ही personal questions हैं. इनको पढ़ कर तो हमें कोई मार के भगा देगा," I told him.

He smiled, "Don't worry, I will give you an official letter signed by me जिससे पता पड़ेगा कि यह सब तुम मेरे behalf में कर रहे हो."

One of the things that I always enjoyed was to snoop into others' private lives (perhaps because my own life had been quite eventless and boring). "This project was an excellent opportunity to nose around in strangers' private lives," I thought.

"तो फिर ये कबसे शुरू कर दें?" I asked, anxious to get started right away.

"आज से ही, but remember that you are under oath to not share this information with anybody," he warned again.

The instructions given to me were - visit every house in the campus, introduce this project and explain the questionnaire. If possible, collect the filled form then or come back later to collect it. I was not supposed to read the form in their presence unless they needed some advice.

When I returned to the hostel, I did not tell anybody, but perhaps the excitement of learning about people's personal matters was all over my face, because I got many comments like 'अरे गुरु बड़े खुश नजर आ रहे हो, क्या बात है?'

As evening approached, I made myself look presentable, took the stack of questionnaires and hit the road. My routine was to ring the doorbell, introduce myself, hand over the letter signed by Dr, Borwanker, and then give them a copy of the questionnaires. The interesting thing was to watch the reaction of the people reading this form. Some liked it, some were furious and said they will talk to the doctor themselves but asked me to come the next day to collect the forms. Some of them were very positive and expressed that it was a right thing the hospital was doing.

This survey gave me lot of opportunities to visit any house I wanted to visit. I had the knowledge as to what contraceptive Prof G.K. Lal was using or Dr. Chatterjee or Dr. Saraf, and many others. Sometimes I would follow some girls and then when these girls would see me at their houses talking to their parents, they probably would have thought that I was up to some prank or at least I thought that they thought like that. I also remember the daughter of one Mr. Lal. His wife was a nurse in the hospital and Mr. Lal was working at Electrical Lab. His daughter was working for Sita travels located at the bottom floor of faculty building. I hope I am not mixing them up. I had collected enough information about our campus's population and knew so much about them that some of my close friends started calling me an encyclopedia.

Coming back to the questionnaires - Some people especially in Type II and I houses would ask me to explain to them in Hindi and request me to fill the form and they will sign. I can recall several interesting interactions with many, and in the light my oath to secrecy I cannot reveal too much but I am dying to share on episode that still makes me crack.

I rang one doorbell. A middle aged woman (perhaps in her late thirties) answered the door. I politely introduced myself and handed her the letter from Dr. Borwanker. She glanced at the letter and proceeded inside to call her husband. I greeted him as he came out (his name is concealed). He invited me in his house. As we both sat down he started to read the questionnaire. Unlike how others had reacted to the questionnaire, this gentleman was quite calm. After going over the questionnaire, he handed over it to me and asked me to fill it for him.

"जी मैं कैसे भर सकता हूं, जवाब तो आपको ही देना पड़ेगा," I told him politely.

"जवाब मैं ही दूंगा, आप सिर्फ इसको भर दीजिये," he clarified.

I read out the questions to him and filled in the answers he gave. To cut the long story short, let me jump to the important questions.

"आपके कितने बच्चे हैं?"

"दो"

Having dealt with this questionnaire several times, I was now an expert. I could ask questions even without looking at the questionnaire. "आप ४० साल के हैं और आपके सिर्फ दो ही बच्चे हैं, आप Family Planning का कोइ method तो use करते ही होंगे," I asked.

"अरे भैय्या Family Planning का तो एक ही तरीका है, और वो है निरोध. मैंने कई बार निरोध के साथ किया, लेकिन मजा नहीं आया. लगता है कि जैसे बरसाती पहन के नहा रहे हो. अब मैंने निरोध use करना बन्द कर दिया है," he revealed.

"तो फिर आप Family Planning कैसे करते हैं?" I probed further.

Friends, I am not kidding; this is what he said - "निकलने से पहले ही तुरन्त बाहर निकाल लेता हूं."

As he said that, his wife walked in with tea and snacks. While sipping the hot tea I looked at him and his wife and could not help myself imagine them naked, executing this delicate and risky family planning maneuver.

I was really enjoying my assignment until one day our hospital got a new chief medical officer Dr (Col.) Dwivedi and then things not only changed for Dr. Borwanker but for me as well; I was put back behind the reception desk making files…

Taken for a ride

It was 1976. The CulFest was still a few weeks away but the campus was already abuzz with activities. The student leaders were in a frenzy to make sure this would be the cultural festival people will remember for a long time. While the handful of IIT girls went into hiding realizing that during the three days of non-stop party the campus would be invaded by many irresistible temptresses, many boys came out of hibernation hoping that their playboy fantasies would be materialized. Learning from the past experience, the campus convenience store had already stocked up on prophylactics. Those chosen to perform on stage were busy practicing their numbers, while the rest researched on the best pick-up lines. Some of us were spending a lot of time in front of mirror trying to find the angle at which they looked the best. The good looking ones amongst us were confident of scoring with the visitors, but the droolers hoped that being chosen as guides for the visitors might be their only ticket to say goodbye to their virginity. One such drooler (identity concealed) was told by somebody that from the front he looked ordinary but his side pose resembled that of Dev Anand's. Throughout the entire cultural festival, he would always talk to girls while looking to his side. Even in the mess when he would see a girl sitting across him, he would turn his face sideways.

One of the most important elements of the festival was the food stall. As the practice had been in the past, the contract for these stalls would be awarded to some seasoned and tested businessman. This year also, the cultural secretary had something similar in mind. But, the quartet of **Ma**, **Mo**, **Ra**, and **Sa** had other ideas.

"Mr. Cultural Secretary, what is the protocol for awarding the stall contract?" asked **Mo**.

"We have invited several restaurant owners and they will bid. The highest bidder will be awarded the contract," replied the secretary.

"Does one have to be a restaurant owner to bid?" asked **Ma**.

"No, anybody can bid."

"What if somebody does phony bidding just to raise the amount?" asked **Sa**.

"Well, if the phony bidder is the last bidder and if he cannot produce the required deposit money, the contract will be awarded to the next highest bidder," clarified the Secretary.

The quartet returned to their rooms realizing that they will never be able to outbid these established businessmen with deep pockets. But they were not going to throw in the towels yet.

A plan was hatched.

At 10'o clock in the morning, it was the day of the bidding. Mr. Secretary and his sidekicks were elegantly perched on the raised dais in the front of the conference room of Hall 1. There were already four teams of businessmen - one of them ran the Hall 5 canteen (I believe his name was Nair), and the remaining three seemed like they came from Kanpur. From the appearances and demeanor of these businessmen, they looked like they were well-fed and had been doing this for years.

A few seconds before the bidding started, the quartet entered the room and headed to the very back. Those present in the room casually glanced at them not thinking much of them.

After asserting his authority via an opening speech, Mr. Secretary went over the rules of the bidding.

"We are going to award the contract to run the stall which will be located right next to the main pandal. The stall will sell only soft drinks and snacks – no booze. The person winning the bid will have to deposit half the amount today," he added.

After giving a fleeting look at his cronies to make sure they were taking notes and were ready, he announced, "I will start the bid with 200 rupees."

"200 one, 200 two."

"250," called out one of the businessmen.

"300," said the other.

"300 one, 300 two."

As the bidding continued, the quartet split with **Ma** and **Sa** positioned at one corner and **Mo** and **Ra** at the other corner on the back of the room. The bidding had reached to 550.

"600," yelled **Ma** from his corner.

All the businessmen sitting in the front looked back to see where this challenge was coming from.

Mr. Secretary did not appear pleased with non-professionals spoiling a highly structured and professionally run gathering. But, as per the rules, he couldn't do much.

"600 one.." he spoke slowly so as to give others sitting in the front an opportunity to outbid **Ma**.

"5000," shouted **Mo** from the other corner.

"What?" everybody gasped and turned around.

There was a macabre silence in the room.

"Do you realize that you have to deposit half the money today?" warned Mr. Secretary while eyeballing **Mo**.

Mo gave a sly smile and gently nodded.

As much as the others wanted to win the lucrative contract for the stall, paying more than Rs. 5000 for the privilege was too much for them to swallow.

"5000 one, 5000 two...." He looked around to see if anybody would challenge **Mo**.

"5000 three," he declared and struck the gavel on the table.

The secretary was disappointed that the award did not go to somebody already tested in the business, but at the same time he was happy that the final bid was Rs. 5000 which was Rs. 4200 more than what it fetched for the same stall last year.

All the outsiders dispersed feeling pity on our lack of business acumen.

It was the time to play part two of the act.

"Congratulation **Mo**. I will need 2500 rupees. Would you pay by check or cash?" he asked.

"What do mean?" said **Mo**, bewildered.

"I mean you have to deposit half the money right now," said Mr. Secretary, adding a little growl to his voice.

Pretending to be embarrassed, **Mo** said, "I apologize for the confusion, Mr. Secretary. I must have misunderstood you. I thought the money was to be given after the CulFest."

As the secretary's eyes reddened, **Ma** butted in, "Does it mean that he doesn't get the contract?"

"That's correct?" thundered Mr. Secretary, asserting his authority.

"Here are 300 rupees then," said **Ma** quickly flashing a stack of ten-rupee bills, reminding him that, as per the rules, the second bidder should be awarded the contract.

Gawking at **Ma** and **Mo**, Mr. Secretary realized that he had just been taken for a ride.

> PS: *Just prior to submitting this story, we had called Mr. Secretary for his approval to publish this. He graciously agreed reminding us that we still owe the balance of 50% for the stall fee, which still shows as outstanding in the books of Cultural Council, having risen to Rs. 53,952 with accumulated interest.*

You know you're over fifty, if...

You don't care where you spouse goes as long as you don't have to go along.

Dhiraj Murdia

I am sure no one has written about Dhiraj Murdia!

He was a gem of a person with deep knowledge in all activities that he was interested in.

I was in a Design course with him, where we had to form groups and make designs/ projects. I think Prof. Samba Siva Rao (Mech) took the course. An instructor loved by one and all, and the most accommodating instructor for all types of sob stories.

'Design' discussions were actually just official bull sessions, held in the drawing hall. Whenever an instructor came near we would suddenly start discussion on some stupid sketch, which was prepared in the first five minutes of the class, and one guy would suddenly start sliding the slide rule

What amazed me was that this young man knew exactly how many votes were won by each candidate in each Gymkhana election, and who cast them. Wing wise, Hall wise who voted for whom and why? And he never came out of his room except for meals!! He also had inside dope in all 'interesting' activities in the campus!!

Another one again about Dhiraj Murdia...

I think it is about Hall 1 only from the timeline, though the picture in my mind thinks its Hall 3.

Anyway, that's not the point... it's about the Jam gang, and Dhiraj Murdia. Like the Jam Gang had good neighborly, and friendly relations with the other gangs, due to the varied cosmopolitan character of JSR (that's blowing one's own trumpet) like the Ghati Gang, the Raman Chopra Gang, the Bong gang, etc., Of course the ONE MAN GANG namely Prof. Singh was associate member of the Jam gang being from what was in those days undivided State Of Bihar.

Now here is my confusion, whether we were discussing the JP Andolan in Hall 3, which had struck Bihar in a big way, or the imposition of the Emergency, or Hall I towards the end, arguing the benefits of Emergency. Prof Singh's brother was the MP from Chatra in Bihar, and we were riding Prof. Singh on the performance of the Congress, and the political chaos. There were emotional outbursts, which did not affect Prof.

in any way, and he managed to subdue the audience with some fudged up figures, which of course we were not capable of refuting. And though we knew in heart of hearts that Prof was just bulling, but we couldn't prove it. There was a big gathering of people there and all were cursing Indira, the Congress, and the misdeeds of the Govt., and in spite of everything, the situation was about to turn into a fight or at least pillow fight. And then it was Raman Chopra who called Dhiraj (actually went and called him not missed call, remember we had no mobiles... or he was passing by and heard the commotion). Since the bull session was very topical he joined the fun. And by God that was the end of Prof. For every figure of development he had, there was a corresponding figure of misery that Dhiraj put out to him. With every reason the Prof had to impose Emergency, Dhiraj had a counter, on either the law, or the voting in the previous election. One by one he demolished the entire edifice that Prof had built and with every statistic rebutted by Dhiraj, there was a huge applause and uproar, until Prof was forced to accept that the Emergency was a total mistake and retreat to a corner. Of course there was loud cheering for Dhiraj.

And this from a man who never came out of his room, and his reputation was only of Maggu.

You know you're over fifty, if...

People call at 9 p.m. and ask, "Did I wake you?"

71

Hair hair बच गये यार

This story happened near faculty houses. Ashok Aggarwal (Avinash's elder brother), Hemant & Manu (Both prof. GVK Rao's sons) and I were enjoying those lighter moments just before the new session by cracking non-veg. jokes etc. Suddenly we found three freshmen moving around the streets of faculty houses to escape from ragging currently happening in the hostels. We called them and asked few initial questions of standard ragging questionnaire.

Then suddenly there was a female voice screaming from behind, "Do not to rag otherwise I will call the Director." We all turned our faces and found a sexy female in maxi dress, who only wanted to get smart youngsters' attention. Ha! She was Mrs. K.P. Singh. To avoid the consequences we all went inside GVK Rao's house. Hey! "Now all of you pull down your pants". "But sir..sir..ss..s.," stuttered one of the freshers. Then what? Like to perform striptease show in the middle of the faculty houses. All of them opened zips/buttons and let their pants fall down. OK, now you all move from one corner of the house to other like fruit sellers – केला लेलो, आम लेलो etc.etc. Soon the sexy show was on and there after one of them was sent to kitchen for preparing tea. At last tea was on the table for every body.

"Oh f...k! The Director! --run." Dr. Amitabh Bhatacharya and his two associates stepping out of a white Ambassador were seen through the

window and were approaching towards main door of the house. Ashok and I hid ourselves inside the washroom. Hemant opened the door. I whispered from the wash room "Shameless freshers pull up your pants and sit on the chairs like our good friends." They could not zip up and consequently could not stand to greet the Director. Dr. Amitabh entered inside like police and asked whether freshers were inside. Imagine there were seven tea cups on the table and only five persons. The Director asked the obvious question "Where are the two others and for whom are these two extra cups?" Hemant explained that the extra two tea cups were for the expected guests and impulsively offered them (Director & Asso.) tea by picking up our half finished tea cups. So he finally left assuming that there might be misperception by Mrs. K.P. Singh.

Ashok Aggarwal and myself came out of the wash room and all together were greatly relieved - hair hair (बाल बाल) बच गये यार!!

You know you're over fifty, if...

In a hostage situation you are likely to be released first.

73

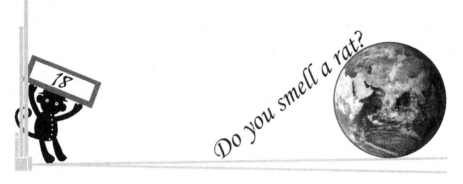

Do you smell a rat?

The year was 1975. The whole campus was euphoric with the anticipation of the onslaught of visitors from across the country. The Culfest was only a week away. The brand new restaurant of Student Activity Center (SAC) with all its glittering furniture and stylish tableware was all decked up and eager to cash in during the three days of non-stop party.

Having won the contract to run the food stall, **Ma**, **Mo**, **Sa**, and **Ra** were also hallucinating with the thought of making a few bucks. **Mo** had already negotiated a great deal with a restaurant owner from Kanpur to provide soft drinks at highly discounted prices. Using his contacts, **Ma** had contracted a cook from Clarks Awadh, an upscale hotel in Lucknow, to prepare burgers.

"साहब ऐसे बर्गर बनाऊंगा कि सब ऊंगली चाटते रह जाएंगे," he assured us.

As things were falling in place, one of us pointed out something that we had overlooked.

"Do you realize that SAC is right next to the पन्डाल?" said **Ra**.

"So what?" asked **Sa**.

"Everybody will go to the SAC instead of coming to our stall?" replied **Ra**, as **Ma** and **Mo** looked on.

"Yes, you're correct. Their prices are competetive, they have better ambience; we will not be able to compete with SAC on quality; we're f…d."

The challenge of competing with SAC turned their jubilation into a serious concern as their dreams of cashing in appeared to be in serious jeopardy. But there was no turning back now.

A plan was hatched.

The plan called for several dead rats. **Mo** volunteered to recruit his contacts in Kanpur to provide the rodents. He purchased several mousetraps and placed them in restaurants in rat-infested neighborhoods of Kanpur, hoping that he would have a plenty of them in a couple of days. To his dismay, none took the bait. "What're we going to do now? The Culfest is only three days away," we panicked.

The next day, we rode a tempo to the city searching for stores specializing in supplies for medical experiments. We found one.

"We are from the medical school. We are conducting a research project for which we need some rodents," said one of us.

Hearing that we were from the medical school, the shop owner perked up.

"We supply all kinds of animals to the medical school. In fact, just last week we delivered five rabbits to Dr. Asthana's laboratory," he said.

"Oh, Dr. Asthana. Yes, yes, we know him," stuttered **Mo**, "But we need the animals for some other project."

Knowing that we knew Dr. Asthana, the owner felt an instant connection with us.

"What kind of animals are you looking for?" he asked.

"Actually, we wanted some rats," said **Ma**.

"Yes, we have rats. I will show you," he said, leading us to a mouse cage containing several rats frolicking in their little space.

"How many do you want?"

"Three or four. How much does one cost?" asked **Va**.

"Four rupees."

We looked at each other trying to sense what the other three were thinking. As we communicated through our body language, the shop owner jumped in, "Since you are Dr. Asthana's students, I will charge only three rupees per rat."

"Do you have dead rats?" asked **Mo**.

"Dead rat? Why do you need dead rats?" he asked, with his eyebrows pulled in.

Finding the other two struggling for words, **Ma** jumped in, "You see, we have already been in medical school for three years but we still get chills cutting open a living creature. So we are hoping that we can get rats that are already dead."

The shop owner smiled.

"अरे चूहे को मारने में क्या डरना, अगर आप लोगों को चूहे को मारने में डर लगता हो तो इन चूहों को मैं मार दूंगा," said the owner as he walked towards the cage.

"अरे नहीं नहीं, Please don't kill any of these," interrupted **Ma**, looking affectionately at the rats who were still prancing around their cage oblivious of our conversation, "Just look at them; how cute and happy they look. Don't you have rats that are already dead?"

Not wanting to miss the opportunity to sell us rats, dead or alive, the shop owner suggested that we put a deposit of 12 rupees and then he will get us four dead rats from his warehouse, which he said was only half an hour away. Agreeing to this deal, we left the store to return after half an hour. As we were leaving, we noticed the rats in the cage looking at us lovingly as if to say – Thank You.

We returned back to the campus with four dead rats hermetically sealed in a plastic bag. Before embarking on our next move, we all

gathered in a room, collected our thoughts, and mentally rehearsed our act.

So as not to be noticed, we ate our dinner right before the mess closed. It was late at night. We arrived separately at the SAC, each carrying a plastic bag. We casually sat at different tables and ordered soft drinks. Each one of us stealthily reached into our bag. Without taking the stuff out of the bag, and, using our fingers' dexterity, we positioned a long strip of masking tape on the corpse. Each one of us then nonchalantly probed under the table ceiling to find a nice flat spot, quietly recited a prayer for the departed soul, and left the cafeteria signaling the other three that the mission had been accomplished.

The Culfest started two days later. We did a roaring business in the stall, charging four times the regular price for the milk shakes, which was 5% milk and sugar, 50% water and ice, and the remaining 45% just plain air bubbles. Nobody complained as they were thrilled to be away from the strong stench coming from the SAC cafeteria.

You know you're over fifty, if...

You quit trying to hold your stomach in, no matter who walks into the room.

Don't piss me off

It was a pleasant Saturday evening in July and I had planned to go home for a function on Sunday. Incidentally, I was the type who would rarely go home on Sundays. Instead I preferred to be in the campus for activities such as, chess, bridge, swimming, table tennis (TT), bull-sessions, night outs, movies; you name it, and I was game.

David Thomas, out of blue, without consulting contesting players, put up a notice on the board that the selections for the Institute's TT team would be held on the Sunday. Since I was eager for a spot in the team for the institute, I contacted him immediately and requested him to do the selection not before 5 pm to allow me time to return to the campus. He graciously agreed.

Eager to show my TT prowess, I reported at the TT room of Hall V at dot 5 pm on Sunday, only to be informed that the selection was over. I was mad as hell and could not sleep the whole night, the bad weather and no lights adding to my rage.

In the morning I headed straight for the TT room not knowing what to do. I kicked at the locked door a few times. Revengeful and still furious, I returned back to the TT room with a hockey stick. Looking around to make sure that nobody was there within the combined radius of the hockey stick and my stretched arm, I aimed at the lock and swung the stick as hard as I could breaking the lock in just one hit.

I called a माली and together we put the table on the trolley which the माली brought from his den.

I said, "बढ़ाओ." He asked, "किधर." I said, "कहीं भी तुम बढ़ाओ." Turning through Hall III side road, then right all the way to the swimming pool, then left across the hospital, I was by now getting tired.

"चलो बाएं गर्ल्स हास्टल की तरफ ले लो," I instructed the mali. Luckily Renu was there. I did not tell her the truth. Instead I told her that this is Institute's Table No. 1 and David Thomas had sent it. I asked for a receipt but she was too scared and anyway she did not have the authority, which rested with the warden, Miss. Usha Kumar.

I right away proceeded towards the faculty building and knocked on her door.

"Yes, please come," she responded. As I peeped in, she said, "You did not come for the 8.30 class."

"Madam, it is more important than that," I replied.

She looked at me inquisitively. What can be more important than the class? I told her the whole story, minus a few important details, requesting for a receipt. She listened to me patiently with that typical smile on her face.

"Well, I think I have not met you," she said.

"Yes madam, I understand but can you ensure the table stays and is not stolen."

She looked at me quizzically (I too am good at ENGLISH, thanks to company of PA) and waves me off.

For two weeks the entire security team along with David Thomas kept looking for the table. It was not a joke - Table No.1, the brand new one, was missing. AND voila, one evening DAVID THOMAS walks in the girls' hostel to meet his friend only to find the girls playing on the Table No. 1.

As expected, he lodged a complaint. The table was duly returned to Hall No. V. The girls were promised another good table otherwise the warden would not let this one go. The girls had a last laugh. I was in deep trouble.

The in-charge of SAC committee was AS and he too was selected in the team on that very fateful evening.

He demanded that I be rusticated. I tendered an unconditional apology. Miss Usha Kumar supported me in the SAC meeting. ALL is well that ends well - not yet my dear.

A week down the line I choose my own team and officially challenged the Institute's team by putting the challenge on the notice board, DAVID THOMAS had no choice but to accept. The entire institute was present in Hall V to watch the match. It was 3x3 total three players, each side playing the other three in rotation.

I had Prakash Mulbagal with me, the best defensive player who would just keep returning the ball tirelessly till the opponent makes a mistake. Gowrishankar, the chess champion, did not know much of TT but I had to practice with him. He played with a Chinese grip and could play anywhere on the table with a straight face.

I was an aggressive player with top spins on forehand and backhand both. I will not go into too much of nitty gritty and technicals.

The first match was between me and Arun Shukla. I was adept at dropping the ball too close to the net on either side and AS did not know how to counter that. The match was over within 15 minutes me winning 2-0.

Next it was Mulbagal vs David Thomas. David was a bit nervous and started playing defensive. Mulbagal won 2-0 and we were up - and a nice applause from the audience. In walks Miss Usha Kumar. A chair was offered to her but she preferred to watch standing. PA beat Gowrishankar hands down. We were still 2-1 up. Even if PA won all three I needed to three off AS or David, and two from the other. The fourth game was between me and David Thomas. I did not find much difficulty in beating him. The score now was 3-1 in our favour. The crowd was now cheering us. Surprisingly, Gowrishankar next defeated AS, who could not get the hang of the Chinese grip. We were now 4-1 up. PA next defeated Mulbagal with his attacking style of banging the feet on the floor. SCORE----4-2. David Thomas next defeated Gowrishankar; score 4-3. Mulbagal next played AS and me. PA was supposed to play the last match. That was not to be because Mulbagal beat AS 2-1. We won 5-3 and the news went all around like a wild fire.

Of course all three of us had to spend a lot of money treating our friends at our own expense. The sad part being that I stopped playing TT after this episode.

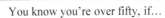

You know you're over fifty, if...

You use your cell phone purely to make and receive calls.

Here's my story. It was 1976 I think and about 40-50 of our batch decided to see हीरा-पन्ना in some theatre in Gumti No 5 area. All was well till the movie ended after midnight. Then things began to happen. Anu Gaf, inspired by the movie, was walking like Dev Anand-tilting to one side-and singing very loudly, "अन्नू की तमन्ना है कि पन्ना उसे मिल जाये......." However a cop on duty who did not like Dev Anand types saw red and

ordered a लाठी charge and hit Anu on the knee with his लाठी. Immediately Anu started sounding like Anu, "अईऊऊऊ, साले नें घुटना तोड़ दिया". And all hell broke loose. The staid IIT-ian and there were about 50 of them were roused out of their bourgeois stupor and transformed into fire breathing revolutionaries baying for the blood of the oppressors. It seemed like Paris 1968 in Gumti No 5 but the cop magically disappeared into thin air.

Many things happened. Sanjiv Sahay made a speech. Takru decided to display his knowledge of police procedure and threatened a cop with section XXX and told him he was the DM's son. Finally around 3 am the cop apologized to Anu and Sahay declared the revolution successful. It was time to go back home - to Kalyanpur.

That night I finally understood the true meaning of the phrase 'Necessity is the mother of invention.' There were about 30 of us left but only one tempo available. And we managed to squeeze in and make it back to IIT. How it was done is still a sweet mystery to me.

You know you're over fifty, if…

You go to a five star restaurant and are content to order just daal chawal instead of murgh musallam.

A self-fulfilling prophecy

Have you heard about Self Fulfilling Prophecy...?

You should not just utter something that you don't want to happen to you, really....

It was the beginning of second semester (I forget the year), and the day of registration. There was nothing to do so it was important to go to town and see movies. But the majority had come back recharged from home, all well stocked up, and they had nothing to buy, and they were also looking at last semester's results, and most had decided to start studying from that day itself, like a new year's resolution !!

So who would go to town, it could only be the biggest fatrus in college. And so who are the most incorrigible, most beyond redemption, and most बिन्दास फतरू? Difficult to guess, except for I, me, myself, namely Mukesh Anjaria. The other two were a class apart, really फतरू but not apparently so...and we didn't care, because they were foreigners...

We have forgotten them, and one is probably no more, but then he was a great friend. To end the suspense, the grand फतरू team comprised of me, Dilip Manucha, and Bharat Raju 'Tojo'. We landed up in Kanpur, with the avowed intention of shopping, movies, & dinner preferably between movies. For shopping, we got down at Parade before बड़ा चौराहा, the idea was to pick up some things, and move on to a theatre, or walk down the mall etc.

Dilip was as usual wearing a coat (blazer) Togo was wearing a sweater and I had something like half sweater or whatever which was inappropriate, inadequate for that month.

So as we got down and started walking, Dilip put his hand inside his blazer pocket and came out with a TOOTHBRUSH! Why should someone carry a toothbrush in his blazer beats me, but a possible explanation was that he slept in that damn garment, and morning brushed his teeth and rushed out to wherever he wanted to go.

So he proudly announced to Togo, "Hey, I've got a toothbrush, we can stay the night in town somewhere!" Togo repeated the discovery to me, and I said "Aw Shucks what a joke?" or something"

So we continued, saw a movie, had lots of stuff to eat Fu Tu, not Chung, after all I was in the company of foreigners, and were actually planning to go back, and went to Bada Chuaraha to get back to IIT. But I convinced them that real men would see two movies when they came to city, and so we went to the second movie.

And, fully satisfied we came back to बड़ा चौराहा, and grandly ensconced ourselves in a Tempo. And we sat and we waited, and we sat and we waited, but no one else came forward to go to Kalyanpur ITEE.

We tried to negotiate some deal with the टेम्पो वाला, but no dice. The last he agreed was Rawatpur. Of course all this drama was happening after the night show we were at 0115 in the morning by the time he agreed, and Togo was cursing Manucha, you and your bloody toothbrush!

Anyway, we got down at Medkal Kalej, Civil Asptaal, or was it Rawatpur? or both are same.... and started searching for alternate transport! And by God, the temperature had fallen; we were quite cold, by then.

85

But wonder of wonders, we could find a cycle rickshaw, who was willing to come the balance 10-12 km for the huge sum of Fifteen or Twenty five Rupees! So we piled in and began the seemingly endless journey. Till the city limits it was alright, we were only fucked, but when we entered the open areas, we were totally rammed. The slight breeze froze us, we or at least I did not have gloves.. then we asked the rickshaw वाला, if we could drive the rickshaw. I mean what the hell we weren't getting anywhere anyway, we were likely to die of hypothermia, and so now was as good a time as any to learn a new trade! No policemen, no traffic, no lights, no worries about the future because it was not visible anyway!

So we took turns trying to drive the rickshaw. I failed miserably, because the rick chain drives only one wheel, the other wheel is a free wheel. So essentially, unless you are able to execute massive compensating force on the front handle, the rick can only travel in circles by pedaling. A great discouragement to novice thieves, and bank robbers planning a quick getaway through narrow lanes (Otherwise the vehicle would require a differential gear mechanism to execute turns - a practical lesson which we couldn't fathom in E.Sc 315).

Dilip anyway didn't have too much stamina, so he didn't manage much, but Togo, did a couple of kilometers with our prodding and गालियां, and I sat merely freezing in the seat. The attempts to drive were necessary to maintain circulation, too. Finally, we handed over to the rickshaw वाला and he got us safely into the campus.

And, by about 2:30 am, we reached the hostel, too numb to even pee. And then the toothbrush वाला turned saviour, he brought out a coil heater or something, which we hung from a chair. His roommate Samuel Joseph upturned his bed and hid behind it saying he wanted to be safe if the damn thing blew up! It took about ten fifteen minutes for each of us to regain sensation in our limbs.

Finally at about 3:00 am, we retired to our rooms. I don't remember if Bharat Raju and I were roommates then or we woke up Munna and Rege. There were constant changes between Me, Munna, and Togo because Togo had the nasty habit of standing on his head early in the morning wearing only a multicolored brief, and if you opened your eyes at dawn you would see a blue and purple printed चड्डी hanging upside down in midair, the rest of him wasn't visible in the dark, and that was scary....

For a week after that, I brushed my teeth with my finger only and avoided Dilip Manucha, unless he would make any other damn prophecy!!!

I remember only 3 roommates of myself, Rege, Munna, and Togo. Rege was our neighbour, and he also had a succession of roommates, Nagi, Munna, Togo, Ratan Choudhry, and {one of the Ghati gang} were in a constant state of flux, and I think that was possible because sometimes some people shacked up 3 in a room, or perhaps because Togo had disappeared for some time....

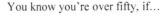

You know you're over fifty, if...

You prefer to hang around your home in dhoti/pajamas because your pants and belt are grating into your carbo-belly.

A super cop

B was the darling student of **Dr. S**. He was very fast in making isometric drawings and was doing exceptionally well in the first year mechanical drawing courses as he already had mechanical drawing as a fifth subject in school. From time to time, Dr. S did not hesitate to appreciate and also involved him in checking and guiding laggards.

That was the most unselfish of times for us because hardly anyone was egotist enough to wish to do his own thinking. There were always so many ready and eager to do it for us. **D** being philosophical & romantic by temperament, his mind was more inclined towards expressive drawing of visual arts. Technical drawing needed unambiguous communication in the preparation of a functional document which he did not appreciate. During self-introspection, he normally justified his not so good performance by arguing that artistic drawings are subjectively interpreted; their meanings are multiply determined. Technical drawings are understood to have one intended meaning only and therefore, boring.

In search for a savior, he got in touch with **B** and struck a deal for the end-semester exam. **B** was sailing high on his reputation and eagerly agreed to help **D** in the exam - A man is always stronger while he is making his reputation than he is after it is made. It was decided that **B** will make isometrics for **D** while he will do some remaining drawings for **B**. It was a simple barter system. Three sheets were provided for three questions and they switched one sheet after completing the work and it was done cleanly. They walked out of the exam hall visibly satisfied for having done the exchange flawlessly.

B could not believe his eyes when he saw 'B' written against technical drawing in his grade sheet on the notice board. He crosschecked with **D.** He had an 'A'. This is sheer injustice. He barged into Dr. **S**'s room to challenge him.

"Sir, I have got B," he said, looking straight into his eyes.

"You deserve it. Your drawings cannot be so shabby. Tell me how you managed them and that too in only one of the sheets?" pat came the reply.

"Sir, I was not well that day," replied **B** a little taken aback, searching for an escape route.

"Trying to be smart is a treacherous art. It is perhaps the only weapon with which it is possible to stab oneself in one's own back. If you argue any further, I have to do detail investigations," said Dr. **S** in a firm voice.

The only choice left for **B** was to run. "Thank you, Sir," he said and left.

Few semesters later..............................

With so many interesting things to do, **B** was slowly losing interest in studies. To optimize his study time, he was looking to select easy & high scoring electives during start of 6th semester. Somebody suggested 'Vibrations' as it had an open book exam. No mugging required. With slight intelligent thinking you can find correct answers from the book during the exam.

With all sincerity, **B** was waiting in one of the front seats for first class of 'Vibrations' to start. He was not aware of the course coordinator. Suddenly, somebody greeted him "Welcome, **B**." **B** looked back. A shiver ran down his spine – Dr. **S** was looking at him with a weird smile. He stood up, and said with an embarrassing look "Thank you, Sir".

B had decided after his past experience with Dr. **S** that he will avoid all future contacts with him at any cost. But unknowingly he was now in his den. 'मरता क्या ना करता' he was left with no option but to cow-down to rebuild his lost reputation with Dr. **S.** He started attending classes regularly. All the lectures were going above his head. He was scoring ducks in the surprise quizzes despite frantic book-searching during the exam and it was not comforting enough for him to know that the class average was 4 out of 20.

Dr. **S** was smart enough to design problems outside the limitations of our knowledge & understanding of the subject. It was like playing cats and mouse with young minds. He was generally a victor. **B** was not ready to take this lightly sitting down. Through contacts, he found out that one of his PhD students (**P**) was helping Dr. **S** in setting up the mid-sem exam paper. With help of **P**'s neighbor, the question paper was carefully sneaked out.

To err is human – but usually a much better excuse is demanded. **B,** as if to regain his reputation once for all, solved all the problems correctly in half the time. And then handing over his answer sheets to Dr. **S** said, "Sir, the questions were not very tough this time." Dr. **S** shook his head in affirmation.

B was waiting anxiously for his answer sheet. It was announced that the class average was 25% better this time and stood at 5. After the distribution of answer sheet was completed, **B** realized he has not got his. He stood up and reminded Dr S that he has not received his paper. "Please come to my room after this class," ordered Dr. **S**.

B followed him to the room, thinking to get a great and special appreciation for his performance.

"I will be instituting an enquiry commission to probe how you got full marks. I know your capabilities," barked Dr. **S.** The moment this was said, **B** realized he has been caught – pants down.

From that day onwards, **B** never attended any of Dr. **S** lectures, refused all attempts by Dr S to contact him as he knew he will get trapped, and dropped the course. Thereafter, the sight of Dr. **S** was enough to make him run.

If **B**'s worst enemy was given the job of writing his epitaph, he couldn't do more than write "He seen his opportunities and took 'em".

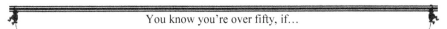

You know you're over fifty, if...

You're the first one to find the bathroom wherever you go.

Wait! I'm also coming

Fortunately this too happened on a Saturday.

I was going to the city when I smelled something cooking in Chedda's room. VERY VERY reluctantly they told me of their plans to go to Kathmandu. "Okay guys see you tomorrow on the train; buy my ticket too," I said.

Right on the dot I boarded the train, only to find nine faces looking at me strangely as if I was a ghost. Not caring about their sentiments, I settled down for the most unpleasant trip, about to unfold.

I was the first to see the TC coming in our bogie. I was aghast to find that I was actually travelling without ticket as these guys did not believe I would show up. Anyway, I was used to these kinds of TC's. I knew the guy would not be able to spot whether we were nine or ten. Away he went happily. If my memory is not failing me we were travelling in an ordinary second class which needs no reservation. I suggested that we at least occupy top six berths. I had to patiently explain to them that lower seats shall be full as the train enters Bihar, and if some of us wish to sleep then it has to be upper berths. Good that they listened to me.

One station before Viratnagar, where we were supposed to unboard, my courage gave away; what if I was caught at Viratnagar; that

would surely eat into my pocket heavily. So I went out of the station and bought myself a ticket to VIRATNAGAR. I had to run to board the train as stoppage was only for a few minutes. And these guys were wondering where I had gone.

NEXT SCENE---

A few of us were on top of a bus and a few inside. After ten hours, Doshi started feeling really cold sitting on the roof. He wanted to get inside but the driver could not hear him. Remember he had that soft voice. I was in no mood to help Doshi for the reason below. LOOOKING BACK - HOW FOOLISH OF ME.

YES, in the train Chedda, Doshi, and Alok indirectly made me play bridge (a game I had never played before. Like a fool I thought it is just another card game). It took me close to eight hundred bucks before I realized that I had virtually no clothes in my suitcase which I was planning to buy in Nepal.

I had already contacted my friends and had worked out a deal in advance for eight beds and two extras in a dormitory type of motel. The guy was waiting for our arrival at the station. J.P. Singh just would not listen or was it Manjeet Singh? They decided to go and have a look on their own. Finally after about two hours they returned with porters and told everyone the room was booked. Okay, I told my guy to lay off and anyway since I had not paid any advance it was easy. Somehow we managed a 18x12ft room with old stinking mattresses, and just one bathroom. No space for movement in the night with ten guys of IIT/K sleeping with their legs moving around in all directions. One look and I knew it was sheer trouble; which was confirmed, in the morning.

Half of us waited to piss while the other half moved in and out of the toilet doing their stuff.

Anyway by ten we were all ready and had breakfast in the market. Next, everyone wanted to go site seeing; all nine wanted to go together on rented bikes; the rent being Nepalese Rs. 40. I had other ideas. I had no clothes for the next day. I actually wanted to go shopping in the evening; hence it was important for me to finish the tour early. So I opted for a taxi. Surprisingly 4 of them joined me. So off we went only to meet the other five on their bikes on the road loooooooking tired at about 5pm. I did my shopping and came back to our room only to find that the buggers did not leave any space for me to lie down. Not to give in I squeezed in.

NEXT DAY THEY WERE ALL IN TAXI _____HA, HA, HA,

The taxi had a heater and after getting wet in the rains it felt really nice and looked like for the first time everyone felt grateful. The next few days went easy; we visited Pokhara and other sites and had fun playing bridge, drinking beer etc. etc.

One day before departure, we all went out for our last shopping spree. I was in a general store and I liked a pack of plastic cards. They were a rarity in Kanpur those days. Suddenly, the lights went off. I could not resist myself whacking it off. I quickly came back to our place and hid the pack of cards and went back to the market. The shop keeper and his men were looking for me and voila they did frisk me. AND when they did not find anything they let me go. I remember meeting a friend of mine from SCINDIA who came out of nowhere in the shop and was just a tourist trying to convince them that it had to be someone else. I could see in their eyes they were not convinced.

SCENE NUMBER TWO

We were all moving in rickshaws towards the border. At the customs, I could sense trouble so I got down and told my rickshawwala that in order to save time it would be better that he crossed the border without me and meet me on the Indian side. I was ready to forego all my purchases rather than get caught with that pack of cards. Luckily for me my man crossed safely as the customs got busy FURIOUSLY frisking all my friends from IIT/K. I lost all contacts with them. At the train time I was on the platform. I opened my suitcase and spread my bed sheet. Suddenly I saw two pandoos enter the compartment and started checking. These were Indians cops. I calmly walked out and left my suitcase open. All my stuff was between those two sheets which looked one. I had carefully strewn them together (THE ONLY WORK DONE SO FAR IN MY LIFE ____THE STICHING THAT IS ____ I am sure Pramila, my wife on reading this story, is definitely gonna give me more of household work).

This time too I did not have a ticket. All tickets were with Chedda and he was nowhere in sight. No TC came till we crossed the Ganges Bridge. It was a magistrate checking. I was stunned. On telling him that my friends have the ticket, he told me to get down and look for them. As luck would have it, some others too were looking for Chedda. We found him. We came back to our compartment and showed the tickets to the magistrate. There was this frail looking guy who had actually slid under the seat and was travelling without ticket. We concealed him from all sides. May be we did good to him, good was returned to us. (THE MORAL OF THE STORY)

I went straight to my home exhausted and hit the bed while these guys went to IIT.

EPILOGUE_____

It seems that they were all frisked and treated very badly. The customs in Nepal kept asking them about me. All their stuff was confiscated or heavy duties were levied. Till date I did not have the courage to tell them that I was the culprit; and they were unnecessarily screwed up because of me. If only they knew the real reason - साले बहुत बम्प मिलते. अल्लाह जाने क्या होता आगे.

You know you're over fifty, if...

You kmow that you're not grouchy; you just don't like traffic, waiting, children, politicians...

Prof. got drunk

The story is particularly remembered for the time we got Prof Singh, alias Ashok Kumar Singh roaring drunk.

As it happened Prof started off his IITK life as a teetotaler, and generally looked down upon those mere mortals who liked to imbibe.

Our response on such occasions was 'you have no clue, since you do not drink'. By the time one was in the final year, Prof., with some encouragement from the 'फतरू s' had 'tasted nectar', but still looked down upon us because according to him, it did nothing to him, and hence was a waste of money.

It may be mentioned that on quite a few occasions one had attempted to get him drunk, but Prof. could put away amazing quantities of the good stuff (beer/rum/whisky/tharra) with no effect whatsoever. Needless to say, since our attempts were 'fueled with our meager allowances, these did not last long.

As it happened, one summer (it was probably the final year) one of my school friends Sanjay Agarwal landed up in Kanpur, and decided to call on me. He was working with HCL, and had come to Kanpur on work. I remember that Vikas, Prof, and I were in L7 watching a movie when he landed up, having found out where we were.

He was staying in some shady hotel near the Kanpur railway station and had some booze lying in his room. Well that was incentive enough, Vikas, Prof, and I piled on, and on the way to his hotel picked up a few bottles of beer. We had also informed Sanjay that there was no point in wasting the booze on Prof, since it didn't affect him (why else should one drink?). Sanjay then decided to challenge Prof to drink a few beer chasers (we had no clue then what these were), and still remain sober. Prof obliged, polished off quite a few, and seemed none the worse initially. Sanjay, suitably impressed suggested that we round off the evening with dinner at Chung Fa, and so all four of us got on a rickshaw, generally high, except for Prof who was still sober.

I think, it was somewhere near Bara Chauraha, that Prof suddenly fell off the rickshaw, and when we stopped and got down to help him, we found Prof roaring drunk, and rolling on the road. That was a sight for our sore eyes. Needless to say, Prof never ever admonished anybody for drinking, having suddenly discovered its virtues!

You know you're over fifty, if…

You are sure that everything you can't find is in a secure place.

The year was 1975. The Allahabad High Court had ruled that Mrs. Indira Gandhi misused her powers for election purposes. The court declared her election null and void and unseated her from her Lok Sabha seat. Soon after that, Mrs. Gandhi proclaimed emergency bringing the democracy to a grinding halt. The Rashtriya Swayamsevak Sangh (RSS), an organization seen by Mrs. Gandhi as being close to the opposition was under a special scanner. All its key leaders were rounded up and jailed. Among the RSS leaders scooped up from the IIT/K campus was the towering Dr. Babu Lal Dhoopar, our Dynamics professor.

The year was 1977. The emergency had just been lifted. The jailed leaders were being released to a crowd of supporters carrying marigold garlands. The frail looking Prof. Dhoopar waved to the crowd and became an instant celebrity in the campus. After the dust settled and the classes resumed, Prof. Dhoopar went back to teaching the Dynamics class. The long imprisonment did remove several pounds off him, but it didn't dent his resolve to rid the society of all its evils.

Fascinated by his persona, I enrolled in his class. Two of the evils that Dr. Dhoopar was determined to eliminate from IIT campus were – people coming late to classes and people skipping classes. In fact, he would require that everybody in his class sat at their assigned seats so if there was any empty seat he would immediately know who the missing person was.

The absconders would be grilled by him in the next class. It had been about two weeks, and I was always on time and never missed any of his classes.

Then shit hit the fan. After one of his classes, I stood in front of the department office in the Faculty Building, with a pen in my hand, absorbed in reading the announcements on the notice board. There were announcements on the upcoming seminars, employment opportunities, research projects by different faculty, upcoming movies in L7, etc. At the corner of the notice board, there was a letterhead pinned to the board by thumbtacks. The letter was signed by Dr. Dhoopar. It caught my attention not because it was from one of my teachers but because some smart ass had struck the word 'Dhoopar' and overwritten on it 'Chootar' and also right underneath he wrote its Hindi translation - 'चूतड़.' Finding it amusing, I chuckled. As I admired this person's creativity, I felt gusts of heavy breathing over my shoulders. I turned around. It was as if somebody had removed the floor from underneath of me. I felt like a matador dressed in bright red, without any sword, standing in front of a raging angry bull. It was Dr. Dhoopar looking down on me with his nostrils flaring and blood in his eyes.

Not knowing how to react, I timidly smiled.

"You are really proud of yourself, aren't you?" he thundered.

I immediately felt a sensation of warm fluid wetting my underpants.

"Sir, I didn't do this," I said submissively.

Even before I could finish my sentence, he erupted looking at the pen still in my hand, "I know very well who did this. Chaps like you are disgrace to this fine institution. You should go home and do something useful with your life instead of wasting your parents' money."

I wanted to tell him again that I didn't do it but no words came out of my mouth; I gagged.

He eyeballed me disdainfully and stomped off.

"What just happened?" I wondered, "This is what they call being at the wrong place at the wrong time."

I was so frightened of Dr. Dhoopar that I did not go to his class the next day. Then came the class after that. As I picked up my notebook to go the class, I shuddered, "Now I am in even deeper trouble. First, he thinks that I insulted him by calling him Dr. चूतड़, and on top of that I am now guilty of missing his class." Being doubly frightened, I skipped the second class. When it came time for the third class, I tried to muster courage to finally face him. But as soon as I thought of those fiery eyes, those flaring nostrils, and my urine-soaked underwear, I trembled. I missed the third, fourth, fifth.....

Reminiscing back, when I look at the first 'F' in Dynamics in my transcript, I fondly think of Dr. Dhoopar, but I wonder why I still feel the wetness deep under.

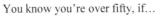
You know you're over fifty, if…

You smile all the time because you can't hear a word of what others are saying.

During those times, it was considered courageous for any girl to challenge the superiority of man's intelligence. Life was tough for them. Their principal job was centered on dealing with family & men. Miss **Re**'s school was located near Chung Fa, the regular mastic joint for IIT crowd. She considered them as decent guys. Living in a joint family and looking for some freedom, she decided to join IIT. Her parents were not happy as they wanted her to opt for regular bachelor's degree in science or arts, being enough to find a suitable match for her as soon as possible.

Re realized in the first year itself that joining IIT was a wrong choice. Nothing in CNR Rao's lectures was so astonishing for her as the amount of ignorance it accumulated in the form of inert facts. TA101, being her specialization now, was the worst.

She was taken by surprise in one of the TA101 class when a red rose appeared on her desk while she was gone to submit her drawing sheet. She looked around, could not find anybody with a slightest interest in her or the rose. To play safe, she picked her T-square and left the rose to wilt away on the table.

In one of the get-togethers – 34 years later – one of the batch mates identified himself as the rose giver and admitted his prank. Touched by the gesture, she advised him "Next time you decide to leave a rose try starting

with a yellow or a white one – so much easier to accept things offered by human hand (no need for calling cards either) rather than things which appear from nowhere. The red rose should be only..............used with discretion".

If the rose-giver had revealed his identity before making a graceful exit from IIT, it would have added zing to the boring classes and some entertainment for both. Perhaps, this thought crossed both the minds, simultaneously.

It was during the third year that it finally dawned on her that maybe she wasn't cut out for engineering and when she broached that with her parents, they were very upset. Being a resident of Kanpur, she would run home for all weekends and also in between, bunking afternoon classes. This flight mechanism only helped in increasing her sense of worthlessness.

Vi was a tennis freak both table and lawn. Somebody had told him that tennis shorts were perfect for his macho looks. Believing what was said, he started playing more of tennis and by the time he reached third year, he had lost all interest in studies. He was privileged enough to be picked up in a car, whenever he wanted to go to his home in Kanpur. In those times, students with cycles were considered well-off.

In one of his car rides back home, he saw **Re** waiting for a lift near SAC building crossing. Lately, he had started hating careless flattery, the kind which exhausts you in your effort to believe it. He wanted an affirmation of his macho looks. This is a chance, he thought. He stopped the car and offered a lift to **Re.** After exchange of initial pleasantries, the conversation reached a dead end. **Vi** posed a grim & serious posture to enhance his macho looks expecting some positive comments from **Re** but in vain. She was in a disturbed frame of mind about her future and preferred to keep quite. Silently they travelled and she took a drop at बड़ा चौराहा.

Thereafter, this became a regular feature whenever **Vi** took a ride in his car back home. He started feeling disillusioned with the हिन्दी movies where he had many a times watched the girl inviting the hero for cup of coffee/tea whenever the hero had given a house-drop to her. He shared this with **VS,** who was helping **Re** to get out of her disturbed state of mind by frequent counseling sessions to her.

"Don't lose faith in yourself and hope for the best," **VS** said, with a comforting voice.

"Hope is all right and so is the faith, but what I would like to see is a little courtesy from her," **Vi** remarked as if asking **VS** to break the ice.

Pouring a little social sewage into her ears, **VS** casually asked **Re** about this mysterious behavior from her side.

"I have two reasons for such behavior – a good reason and the real reason," she explained, "The road from बड़ा चौराहा to my house is a driver's nightmare due to congestion and bad traffic sense. I would not like **Vi** using colorful language whenever his car gets scratched for free –this is the good one."

'Tact is the art of making a point without making an enemy' thought **VS**, and smiled……… She continued "I live in a huge हवेली like complex with over 30 rooms – different sections of this ancestral house is occupied by my grandfathers' family members. If I would have invited him there is every likelihood that a well-meaning uncle or cousin would have probed his family history. I want to spare him from all this झंझट. This is the real one. "

VS thought hard to find a solution of this complex problem. As the picture become clearer, he realized that nature makes boys and girls lovely to look upon so they can be tolerated until they acquire some sense. He roped in both **Re & Vi** for a project work relating to study of "Structures under microscope". Both of them being myopic, **VS** would set the microscope's focal length and then would give them to readjust the focus as per their individual requirements. There was always a fight among them as their focal lengths were different resulting in no readings recorded.

VS was very happy to observe the end result of this project. Now **Vi** could look right at **Re** without seeing her - and **Re** could see right through **Vi** without looking at him.

As **Re** was coming to terms with herself, she was pressurized to get married by her parents – leaving her at an all-time low. She moved to IITB and completed her B.Tech from there.

Her husband left his job and started a business which failed. The monetary loss was huge and the couple was totally devastated. She single handedly took charge - raising her child, taking care of her husband, her frail parents and working with UN. She is now successful by all means.

She returned to IIT couple of times in between to offer short-term assignments to different faculty members. In August, 2011 she was back at the campus to talk to SAID on non-traditional careers and realized that a number of students were facing the same dilemma of low self-esteem. She convinced the students that their fears would never come true and in the real world attitude is far more important than a CPI. So even for five points something CPI there are employment and growth opportunities.

<u>Her Advice</u>: Just trust life, it works out fine for everyone (there are no exclusions). Some of us are slow starters, others have a few more bumps along the way but eventually we all get there. The good thing about getting to the bottom - it takes away the fear of sinking and finding your feet even at the bottom helps you spring right back.

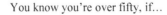

You know you're over fifty, if...

You now spend more time with your pillows than with your mate.

And the winner is...

The year was 1975. The Culfest was in full swing. The food stall was the favorite hangout for the visitors. Boys were in frenzy, especially during the program breaks, throwing money at us to buy our patented watery milk shakes, and crisp mutton burgers to woo girls. **Ma, Mo, Sa,** and **Ra** had to recruit their friends to keep up with the hysteria. While we were all gaga looking at the cash register overflowing with money, the sight of other boys taking liberty with beautiful girls was an eyesore to us.

"We are stuck in the stall here while all these other dudes are realizing their fantasies," said **Sa**. The rest of us nodded.

It was particularly hurtful when we would see a really hot girl with an ugly guy.

"Taking this stall was a bad idea," said **Ra**.

"Yes, you're correct," concurred **Sa**, "If we were not stuck here, we would be with these babes. They're everywhere."

A plan was hatched.

We immediately went to work and designed three big posters. Each poster said the following in big and bold characters:

"WIN FREE FOOD AND DRINKS FOR A DAY"

The posters were hung at visibly most prominent locations on the stall.

No sooner were they up, enquiries started coming in. "So what do I have to do to win this?" asked one dude.

"It's very simple," said **Mo**, handing him over a small piece of paper and a pencil, "Just write your name and your college name on this sheet, fold it, and give it to me."

Pointing to a large cardboard box, he continued, "I'll put it in this box. We will randomly pull names from this box and announce the winners."

Soon the word got around and everybody wanted to be a part of the action. According to the plan, **Mo** would take the folded piece of paper from the hopefuls and hand it over to **Ma**, who would then walk to the cardboard box and put it in. The process would continue seamlessly except when the customer was a hot babe. In those situations, **Ma** would stealthily unfold the paper and read her name before putting it in the cardboard box.

After sometime, the winners' name would be displayed on another board. We would display several names of both boys and girls. The displayed boys' names were phony and of nonexistent persons (such as Pavan Sandeela, Kalpesh Kaminey), but the girls' names were of those hot babes that we had identified earlier. To keep the cultural secretary off our backs if in case he got the wind of our scheme, we made him also the winner of the prize (he was the only real non-female winner of the prize).

Having put the bait, now all we had to do now was to sit and wait. When a girl would approach to claim her free-food-free-drink prize, one of us would become the liaison between her and her prize. We had already made a deal amongst ourselves as to who will entertain which girl(s) except for some girls all three of us wanted to be the lead liason. Those conflicts were quickly resolved as there were plenty of girls to choose from. This game continued for three days well into the wee hours of night. One thing led to other, and you can guess the rest of the story.

We took turns humoring, entertaining, and ....these babes.

We had only heard of the sayings, "शिकार शिकारी के पास आता है" or "कुआँ प्यासे के पास आता है," but that day we were living them.

Thank you, IIT!   Thank you, Culfest!!!!!!!!!!!!!!!

You know you're over fifty, if...

You realize that the last time you were inside a woman was when you were inside the Statue of Liberty.

108

The green monster

No one has talked about the Singapore Surd, Jasbir Singh Judge!

He was a Green Belt in Karate. Shall we call this story "The Green Monster?" Actually he was a nice guy, except for the Green Belt thing going to his head...

All of some 51 kg. he considered himself the greatest fighting champion alive. Though he probably was never seen as the Punjabi guy with the 32 inch waist, he was full of Punjabi bravado. "ओये! कौंड़ है वो पैंड़ दा....देख लेंगे साले को! सामने तो आये!" and he was a regular at the Gym, probably because that's where he could show off, rather than in class....?

And he had a year's start on our batch, and though his batch was the largest till that date in any IIT (Yadupati Singhania's batch) no one wanted to take on crazy Surd in any sort of physical match, so he became uncrowned HeMan and the Master of his Universe...

Until, of course a wiry and tough young Punjabi, this time from Burma (now Myanmar) came along to spoil the fun! And of course with an innovative name like Caesar Singh, he was not likely to accept anyone else's domination over him, at least at the physical level. Soft spoken, wouldn't even hurt a fly, well mannered, polite, but no Pangas please. He subjected himself to ragging as much as he could tolerate, all in good fun...

But apparently, Jasbir S Judge got on his wrong side ! He said, "पैंट उतार, नहीं तो मैं उतार दूंगा!" or some such thing.

अब एक सरदार पगड़ी वाला, और दूसरा बिना पगड़ी! हो गया पंगा...

"Oye, you touch me, and I'll hammer you!" was apparently Caesar's reply...

"Yeah, you think you can hammer me, let's see?"

But not today, we'll duel it out in the Gym tomorrow, it was decided, with the intervention of all present, after all no one wanted a batch fight... "साला Fresher Jasbir Singh Judge से पंगा लेता है, उसको तो मैं देख लूंगा, एक दो कराटे की मार लगेगी, अपने आप लाइन पे आ जायेगा साला fresher!"

And so next day, well before the appointed time, Jasbir Singh Judge, in Karate uniform, wearing his famous Green Belt, started warm ups in the gym in Hall I. "आने दो साले को, चटनी बना दूंगा. मेरे से पंगा?" was the refrain... "If he bloody acts funny, I'll bloody kill him!" roared the Singapore lion, "नहीं तो थोड़ी पिटायी करके छोड़ दूंगा!"

'लेकिन बंदा आया क्यों नहीं, फट गयी है साले की! Walkover दे दिया...' and so on. Judge was fretting and fuming, कि साले में दम नहीं था तो पंगा क्यों लिया!

And when jasbir was at the peak of his fury, came the news 'कि वो आ रहा है, दो चार बंदे भी साथ हैं!' लेकिन अपना पहलवान तो बड़ा धीरे धीरे आ रहा था, और Jasbir इधर नाच रहा था 'देख लूंगा, आने तो दे.

And so Caesar and small party made a Grand Appearance a few minutes later... wonder of wonders, he was also wearing a Karateka Dress!! As he came closer, and within sight of Judge, he slowly bent down to the ground touched it, in a prayer before the fight, and slowly took out his belt from the pocket, and put it on, flexed his pectorals, a few reciprocating movements of his elbows outward, a couple of quick leaps to take position, and the Judge came out of the gym, where he was hitting a punching bag.

When he came out, he saw Caesar, and his expression changed... he came in front of him and bowed low, very low, with his hands at his

side, and then with his hands joined across his chest, he bowed again as if to say, "Yes, Master! I am ready for the lesson!" and Caesar acknowledged with just a slight bow! The fight was over even before it started, and the walkover was by Caesar, because Jasbir couldn't possible fight him and hope to win, after all, Caesar's belt was a dark Brown going to Black, and young Sardaar had a beginner's Green belt only to his credit..... the rest, as they say, is History... Jasbir Singh Judge was his assistant in Caesar's karate classes, which by the way I also attended. Of course, only some, like I attend all classes.. only some!!

You know you're over fifty, if...

You receive the same amount of respect that you showed oldies when you were young –
none.

A bullish encounter

On one of the escapades to Lucknow, we (**Mo**, **Bi** & **VG)** were strolling in one of the side streets of Hazratgunj, the main hangout market place of the town. Suddenly a crumpled ball of paper fell in front of us. Looking up to where this projectile came from, we were pleasantly surprised.......A young pretty girl at the second floor window was giggling at us. Instantly we thought it was an invitation to us for something exciting. We smiled back our irritation on the method employed by her. On this she shyly smiled and disappeared inside. Some of the passersby gave a cursory glance at us, trying to figure out what we were up to.

We stood there, opened the paper ball for some sweet message......trying to figure out the meaning of this event. As we held the blank paper and scratched our head, the girl reappeared again and waved at us – we responded. **Bi** took out his little black comb from his back pocket and started putting his hair in order – as if preparing for the next scene. The other two watched him waiting for the comb to be freed. The girl stayed at the window watching our activities.......unsure of our next move.

Suddenly, **Bi** was pushed forward with a great force. To our astonishment it was a साँड़ (Bull)....lazily moving ahead ....**Bi** fell flat on the road. The other two helped him on his feet. The साँड़ stopped and looked back with an expression telling the trio that the girl is mine. **Bi** looked straight in his eyes ......the bull moved on carelessly on his journey.

Feeling embarrassed, **Bi** looked up to see the girl's reaction. To show that that he was not going to tolerate disrespect of an IITian by a साँड़, he ran behind the bull and before anybody could realize what his intentions were, he lifted the bull's tail and punched him in his ass. Bulls are straight forward animals and do not like anybody messing with their behind especially when a pretty girl is around. To show his displeasure, the bull went amok and destroyed everything in its path. There was complete commotion in the market with shopkeepers downing their shutters and people running to get away from his fury.

Like a true Bollywood hero, **Bi** hand reached his shirt collar to make it stand......He looked up.....the girl smiled as if acknowledging his combativeness. **Bi** looked at the other two....with a slight tilt & shaking head ...trying to look like Dev Anand. The market was still in commotion and the bull still on rampage. **Bi** looked up....the girl was nowhere to be seen........the window was closed.

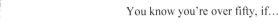

You know you're over fifty, if...

You know there is a younger person in you – wondering what the hell happened.

113

Nothing succeeds like a failure

It was the beginning of second semester of 4th year. Sitting on the front-staircase of the library, **Mo & Ra** were enjoying the cool breeze. The conversation was dull, as is always the case when we are speaking only favorably of ourselves.

Mo said, "I think it is fair to say that my own estimate of myself is at variance with that of some of my faculty. We have to show them."

Ra did not want to comment on this controversial matter, as he knew **Mo** always saw both points of view – the one that's wrong, and his. He probingly asked, "What do you mean?"

"कुछ different करना होगा. अगर CPI में concentrate करोगे तो गांडू बन जाओगे. Job market में बहुत competition है. वहां CPI ज्यादा matter करता है. बाहर जाने की छोड़ो - अंग्रेजो के तलवे नहीं चाटेंगे. When we will come downstairs from this ivory tower, most are apt to walk straight into the gutter. We have to think about some business." Trying to talk **Ra** out of his sober and natural opinions, **Mo** replied.

"ये क्या है? Faculty – CPI – Business," **Ra** asked curiously.

"Army requires Egg Powder for Jawans stationed on the borders. Presently, we are importing. The process is simple – break the egg, separate yoke & albumen and then spray dry them – and the powder is ready. Let us start planning from today itself," explained **Mo**.

Recently, **Ra** had gone to Delhi and had visited JNU. He had come back with the impression that we are unknowingly breaking our heads in solving technical problems whereas the students at JNU are learning how to manage/control these technocrats. He was of the firm belief that parents send their wards to engineering schools to prepare them to become slaves of white masters or brown sahibs. The institute fulfilled their expectations.

Supporting the idea, he remarked "The mechanics of running a business are really not very complicated when you get down to essentials. You have to make some stuff and sell it to somebody for more than it cost you. That's about all there is to it."

After some deliberations, it was concluded that this simple idea lies within the reach only of complex minds – like ours. It was decided that the final year project would be "**Egg breaking and yoke/albumen separating machine**". **Sa** was roped in as the third partner taking into consideration his drawing skills and Prof. G. K. Lal as guide. Proposal was submitted and accepted. One semester was for making detail drawings and next semester for making a working model.

Lot of ideas was thrown around about solutions to the problem of how to break an egg cleanly, keeping the shell out of the mix and the yolk intact. None of the questions which bothered us had an easy answer and many of them had no answer at all. It was decided to consult an 'अन्डा पराठा cook' for expert advice.

Abdulla, the cook at IIT gate, in his late 30's, had an experience of 8 yrs in breaking eggs for अन्डा पराठा. On approaching him for advice, he professed "The shell of the hen's egg consists of a series of layers, whose strength varies according to the health and age of the hen that laid it. There are many factors involved in getting the perfect break – the type of implement, velocity, angle of impact, force and good follow-through motion." We were awe-struck by such clarity of thought reaffirming our belief that the actual ग्यान rested outside IIT.

He continued, "For best result, you should hold the egg in the palm of your hand with the pointed end towards your fingertips. You should then break it with a palette knife, striking it across the middle of the egg using a kind of wrist action used to cast a fly-fishing line. This way you produce pressure high enough to break the shell with minimal cracking on either side of the line of impact – thus reducing the risk of shell in the mix. If people stick to breaking eggs this way their mixes will be shell free. But words of caution – larger eggs have shells more at risk from breaking badly."

"When you have broken shell in your mix, what do you do?" **Sa** asked.

The owner of the Dhaba who was listening to our conversation, cut through and said, "Neatness and dexterity aren't my major selling point, I'm afraid - the day I start worrying about how neatly I crack an egg will be the day I need to be accompanied to a sanatorium."

We felt as if we have suddenly discovered a proven technique which ensures that we can crack an egg in our would-be machine with confidence. Only one month was left for submission of our project report. We immediately moved on to the drawing board. A good report was made but our guide did not feel so and gave us 'B'.

"Sir, the idea is out-of-box and so much effort has gone in making this report. Then why B?" asked **Sa.**

"Your report is basically prejudice and emotions with minimum of substance. Ideas do not count, how you present them is important. Next semester if you are able to make a nice working model, I can give you A," remarked Dr. G.K. Lal in a firm tone. This was like knocking a man into the ditch, and then you tell him to remain content in the position in which providence has placed him.

"Thank you, Sir," we replied in unison and left his room.

It was the first semester of our 5th year and we felt like Dadas ready to conquer the world. Our love for idleness was at its' peak. We loved to busy ourselves with trifles, to begin hundred things and not finish one of them. In short – to fritter away the whole day inconsequentially and incoherently, and to follow nothing but the whims of the moment. The faculty had lost all hope on us to improve. That may be one of the reasons for IITs reducing the duration of the B.Tech. program from 5 to 4 years in 1981. Under this backdrop, we started our model making earnestly.

Since the project was unique, getting it done in the institute workshop was a big task. If it were not for the demands made upon us by the institute, we would have provided living proof that a man can live quite happily for decades without ever doing any work. We decided to outsource the fabrication. With the help of **Mo**'s contacts a fabricator was located near Parade ground. After understanding the project, he agreed to make the model in 3 weeks at a cost of Rs.100/-. We paid him Rs.50/- as advance. A great job done, we thought.

Three weeks later, we went to see our machine – the fabricator was nowhere to be seen and his shop was closed. On enquiry, we came to know that he has gone to his village and would be back after a week. We convinced ourselves that this is a minor abrasion and nothing to worry as the submission date is still 5 weeks away. But in our hearts we knew that 'गोली हो गयी है'.

We walked aimlessly without any conversation. Before we could make out where we are, we were standing in front of a movie hall named 'Capital'. We went inside, and bought balcony tickets for 75p each. To cut costs, the hall management issued tickets by stamping your palm instead of paper tickets. Appreciating this, we took our seats. The seats were movable and could be carried anywhere you wished to sit. The movie started and it was '**Bhoot Mere Sathi**'. We were enjoying a scene where the Bhoots were having a disco party in 'Kabristan'. Suddenly, the reel in the projector snapped and the lights were switched on. The Chaiwalas entered with kettle filled with steaming chai in one hand and a pack of earthen pots (Kulhaad कुल्लढ़) in the other. We bought 3 कुल्लढ़s of tea and while sipping were enjoying the commotion around us. After finishing our tea we looked around for a waste bin. Not finding any, we lobbed our कुल्लढ़s down from our balcony. Did not know where they landed, but immediately thereafter we saw some कुल्लढ़s coming towards us from below galleries. A कुल्लढ़ war had started. We quickly picked ourselves; ran out of the hall and took a tempo back to hostel.

After a week, on reaching the fabricator's shop, we saw him chatting with his friends.

"वो अंडा तोड़ने वाली मशीन कहां है?" asked **Mo.**

"साहिब, थोड़ा परेशानी में था, गांव जाना पड़ा. अभी काम चालू नहीं कर पाये हैं," said the fabricator.

"अरे तुमने तो कहानी कर दी. कब शुरू करोगे?" asked **Sa.**

"बस आज से. दस दिन में हो जायेगा," the fabricator said with considerable confidence.

Being trapped, we had no option but to give another Rs.25/- as advance and declare that if he finishes the job in 10 day he will be given Rs.25/- as bonus.

For the next 10 days, we were there in his shop from morning till evening supervising the making of our beloved machine. In between, we made it a point to see movies.

Finally on the ninth day, the working model was ready. Trials were conducted with roughly around two dozen eggs and we were happy that the success rate of the machine was close to 80%. We paid the balance amount plus bonus and carried the machine to our hostel. Our cost for the machine worked out to be Rs.240/- including conveyance, movie tickets & food. Nonetheless, our spirits were high.

We did some more trials in our room, and to our dismay we discovered that the more trials we took, the egg breaking strike rate reduced. We stopped trials at 40% efficiency. We wanted to get 'A' and this machine's future looked bleak.

Our only hope was now Abdulla. We approached him once again and described the situation. In a tone similar to Ajit (famous hindi movie villain of those times) he said "आप लोग अपनी सोच को उठाओ. हाथी भी अंडा तोड़ने में कभी कभी चूक जाता है," and went into his kitchen.

Soon thereafter, Abdulla was coming towards us with a plate in his hand containing eggs. "ये लीजिये पांच अंडे. इनके छिलके पर गौर फर्गाइये. ये पतली लाइन देख रहे हैं?" We looked attentively and saw a very fine semi-circular crack on the shell.

"अब आप इसे ले जाइये. इसको बस एक हल्का सा तमाचा देने की जरूरत है और आपका काम हो जायेगा," said Abdulla. As a priced possession we carried the eggs suitably packed in an egg tray to our room.

The next day was the demonstration. We were standing in front of an astonished Dr.GKL who was keenly looking at our machine. We could not comprehend what was going into his mind, but from his facial expressions we could make out that a disaster is not far away. It may be unconstitutional, but we always prayed before a test. After a small prayer, the egg was placed in the machine and the springs of the striker (a wedge made of tin sheet) were released for the wedge to move forward and strike

EGG CRACKING MACHINE.

the egg. The wedge struck the egg and the wedge broke. The egg was happily sitting in its position.

"Ask any failure. Success is simply a matter of luck. I have nothing more to say. Thanks & good luck," commented Dr.GKL and moved on to inspect other models. We were shattered. The only comforting factor was that we all were evenly compensated with a D.

119

This setback has never left us and still lingers on somewhere at the back of our mind.

Sa is a successful businessman involved in installation & commissioning of machines. All machines required are outsourced. He never tried to venture into machine building.

Ra is in States, pursuing his PhD in Computational Biology in the hope that someday he will be able to make a biological knife for breaking eggs. He is due to submit his thesis shortly.

Mo was into making machines for many years and now is involved in tightening / loosening screws of God made machines (Humans). For him, the key to everything is patience. He thinks that you get the chicken by hatching the egg – not by smashing it.

You know you're over fifty, if…

You don't avoid temptation – it avoids you.

120

A trip through hell

It was May of 1977. Why would anybody stay in Kanpur in 100 plus degrees Fahrenheit heat? No air conditioning, no water cooler. Well, why not, especially if you have just finished taking your last test, I mean the very last test at the end of the five years.

The main street in front of Hall 1 was packed with 3-wheeler tempos loading up a batch of freshly crowned engineers to the train station as they waved goodbye to those left behind. Some departed in style – they were picked up in Ambassador Cars with a uniformed driver sent by their parents. By afternoon, almost the entire hostel was empty. Only a handful of hard cores who had not yet had enough of IIT stayed behind.

Ma looked down from his third floor room. The streets were mostly empty. He looked into his pocket for a change to buy a cigarette. On his way to the canteen he ran into **As**. "'When are you going home?" asked **As**. "I think I'll hang around here for a few days," replied **Ma**. "Me too," said **As**.

"What're you buggers up to?" yelled **Pr** from a distance.

"You didn't go home?" asked **Ma**.

"F..k the home. I was there this morning. Couldn't take it anymore. I bummed somebody's scooter and came back here," said **Pr**.

"You have a scooter!" both **Ma** and **As** screamed in unison with their mouths open wide, "We can go somewhere."

"You want to go to putrid, squalid, slipshod streets of Kanpur?" said **Pr** showing off his vocabulary prowess, "If you really want to go somewhere let's go somewhere cool."

"How about Naini Taal?" blurted **Ma**.

"Ya right? As if **Pr** has balls to take somebody's scooter to Naini Taal," said **As**.

Enraged, **Pr** couldn't take being challenged like this, "I've bigger balls than yours. Don't propound something that you know you don't have fortitude for."

Pr had this habit of throwing in some words that made you wonder – what did he actually mean?

"I'm ready to go to Naini Taal," said **Ma**, hoping that **As** will cop out.

None of the three had balls to reveal the actual size of their balls.

"I'll come," said **As** casually believing that **Pr** will find some excuse to chicken out.

"OK, let's go," said **Pr**.

All three of us were playing the mind games hoping that one of the other two will crack first.

"Are you serious? Didn't you say that this scooter is not yours and you have to return it today?" said **Ma**.

"Don't agonize yourself on whose scooter it is. Let's go," said **Pr**, standing up pretending to be 6 feet tall.

"Okay, let's go," said **Ma** and **As** together.

They walked to the scooter. **Pr** led, followed by **Ma** and then **As** at the back.

"Are you feeling a little aqueous in your trousers yet," said **Pr**, addressing **As**.

"I'm just fine," said **As**, being confident that this plan would never materialize.

We came to where the scooter was parked. As soon as **As** looked at the scooter, he grinned.

"Look at this beat up piece of shit. It can't take three bulky guys even to Kalyanpur," he said.

"I knew it, I knew it," **Pr** jumped in, "Trying to find excuses, aren't you? You're not pugnacious enough for an adventure like that."

"It's your scooter. It ain't my problem. Let's go," countered **As**.

All of us were trying to buy time hoping that senses will eventually prevail.

"How much money do you guys have?" asked **Ma**.

"I've 42 bucks," said **Pr**. "I've 35," said **Ma**. "I have only 18. Let me go to my room and get some more," said **As**.

"Bugger, I know you. You're running away, aren't you?" said **Pr**.

"No, I'm not running away. We have a total of 95 rupees. We need more money," he clarified.

To raise the stake in the hope that the plan would fall apart, **Ma** added, "The fun part would be reach Naini Taal in this amount."

"OK let's go," all three of them said in chorus.

It was about 6'o clock in the evening. The sun was setting in the clear sky. **Pr** kick started the scooter, which surprisingly started in just one kick. He took the pilot's seat, **As** in the middle, and **Ma** at the back, and off we started our 'Trip through Hell.' But looking back now from the comfort of our air-conditioned houses, the hell was not that bad actually.

Now everybody had accepted the inevitable and the general mood was to enjoy the ride. Our first stop was at Kalyanpur ठेका to purchase two bottles of देसी शराब. Now we had less than 80 rupees left, but who was counting. We rode for a couple of hours until we were in the middle of nowhere. It was time to put some fuel in ourselves. Stopping at the side of the road under starry night, we unscrewed the first bottle and took turns taking swigs directly off the bottle. If there is anything that comes close to having an orgasm, it was this – being insane with your demented friends. While none of us had our dinner but food was the last thing in our mind. We drank and danced on the empty street, occasionally returning to the side to let the trucks pass by. Nobody dared stopped to check on us perhaps due to the fear being robbed by three drunkards. Before we realized it, more than half the content of the bottle had been transferred to our bellies. Its effect on our empty stomach was immediate – an ultimate euphoria. We felt invincible – we could ride the scooter to the moon.

It was time to continue our 'Trip through Hell.' **Ma** took to the helm with **As** in the middle and **Pr** at the rear.

We stopped at a gas station and filled up the scooter. We may have gotten a bite to eat – I don't remember. Back to the road again.

Fast forward to several hours of driving in dark night surrounded by solitary landscape.

While we kept taking breaks to wet our throats with the only fluid that we had, we forgot that a full tank of the scooter with more than 500 pounds of cargo on its seats will travel only a finite distance.

It was about 3 a.m. We must have travelled more than 150 miles by now. We were cruising northwards at a decent speed – then suddenly – we heard the internal combustion engine of our scooter cough, which soon turned into a full blown asthma attack.

"What the hell is that?" we wondered as we pulled the scooter to the side.

Pretending to be an expert in resolving the scooter related technical problems, **Pr** took charge while the other two engineers (yes, we could call ourselves engineers now) looked on. He tried to kick start it several times. When that didn't work, he used the trick of tilting the scooter on one side. That didn't work either. He then tilted it to the other side and shook it vigorously side to side, but again no luck. As we recall that in order for the fuel gage to work the machine had to be turned on, so it was not clear if no-fuel was our problem. One of us suggested peeping inside the gas tank to see if there was any fuel left. It was difficult to see inside the tank in the dark. Our scooter genius **Pr** asked us to put our ears close the gas tank to listen to any splashing sound while he shook the scooter. "There is no sound," announced **Ma** and **As**.

"We're screwed," we all said.

We sat on the dirt on the side of the road, took a few more swigs of ठर्रा, smoked some cigarettes, and pondered on our next move. Then suddenly **As** announced that he had a brilliant idea. "What's it?" asked **Ma** and **Pr**.

"We have one bottle of ठर्रा left," he said.

125

"So?" said **Ma** and **Pr** looking at him irritatingly.

"Both gasoline and ठर्रा are combustible. So we can use ठर्रा as a fuel."

"Do you know what you are talking about?" asked **Ma**.

"Yes, I know what I'm talking about, I had an A in Thermodynamics," said **As** proudly.

His logic did make sense and also since **As**'s CPI was more than both **Ma** and **Pr** combined, nobody challenged him – A BIG MISTAKE.

We took one swig each from the second bottle and emptied the rest into the gas tank. As **Ma** was about to toss the two empty bottles on the side, **As** stopped him, "Don't throw these bottles here. The broken glass may cut somebody. Let's take it with us and we will dispose of them properly."

Admiring his sense of concern for others, **Ma** put the bottles in the scooter pouch in the front. Later on we realized that it was a HUGE BLUNDER.

Since using ठर्रा for fuel was **As**'s idea, he felt responsible for kick starting the scooter. He kicked it a few times – nothing happened. Then he did the same tilting routine – and wow – the scooter started.

There was a spontaneous smile on all our faces. **As**'s face was gleaming with pride. "When daddy talks, children should listen," he said boastfully.

Ma and **Pr** patted him on his back for truly a bright idea.

Off we went again. After about a mile, the scooter coughed again. This time the sound of the cough was different than what we had heard before; it sounded more like a whooping cough. The frequency of coughing increased rapidly and eventually within a short distance it sounded like the scooter was having a tuberculosis attack. CLUNK – CLUNK – CLUNK - and then there was a deathly silence.

"A bottle of fuel can't be finished in just one mile," said **As**.

We stopped and made several attempts to kick start the machine but it didn't cooperate.

"So, what is your next idea, Mr. Genius," said **Pr** sarcastically to **As**.

There we were in the middle of nowhere at about 4 a.m. with no fuel, no booze, no food, nothing. Having no other choice, we decided to roll the scooter by hand, taking turns, to the next town. So there we went again, heading north, but this time one person was holding the handles while the other two were pushing from behind.

Fast forward to about four hours of pushing.

It was early morning and we were in a town. I believe the town was called Hardoi. When we told the mechanic what the scooter had been doing and what we did to it, he laughed and almost pulled his hair. We were too embarrassed to tell him that we just graduated with engineering degrees from our country's premier institution. He looked at us as if we came from some other planet.

"ये क्या कर दिया आपने. अब पूरे एन्जिन की सफाई करनी पड़ेगी." he said.

Pr looked at **As** disdainfully, "So Mr. Thermodynamics, what do you have to say now?"

As quietly shrugged his shoulders.

After paying for the engine clean up, we had about 40 rupees on us. With this money we filled up the tank, ate some cheap lunch of आलू पूड़ी from a roadside ठेला, and now we had only a couple of bucks on us. Nobody wanted to show their effeminate side by suggesting – 'Let's go back now'. So without even thinking, we headed north again.

Fast forward to about six hours of driving.

It was tough as we had no fluid to wet our throats. Then – Eureka – we were in Naini Taal. We were really proud of ourselves that we all made it in one piece. But now, we had no money and an empty stomach and an empty gas tank. How are we going to go back?

127

It was late in the evening. Sitting by the side of road right in the heart of Naini Taal, we looked around the posh hotels around us wondering how lucky the people living in there must be. We could clearly see through the glass window a family sitting in a restaurant biting into roasted chicken leg – it was a pure torture watching them eat.

'How to get some money?' was the question in our mind. "Perhaps we should do some manual labor to earn enough money so we can go back," we thought. But it was too late to approach anybody. We decided to spend the night outside some hotel.

Fast forward to the next day.

It was 10 am in the bright morning in beautiful Naini Taal. Everywhere you looked, there were well dressed tourists; honeymooners holding hands; women in colorful sarees, pants, and in salwar kurta; children happy to be there. We must not have realized it but each of us must be carrying a halo of bad odor emanating from us because we noticed that whenever we talked to a stranger, he/she would twitch his/her nose and subtly increase the distance from us. None of us had brushed, shaved, bathed, or answered nature's call (the major one) during the last 40 hours.

We walked to outside of a five-star hotel and chatted with the uniformed security man hoping that we could talk him into providing us some leftover food. Good thing that our skills to make a friend out of a stranger were still alive and well. We learnt from the security guard that there was a Chamber of Commerce conference in that hotel and that Mr. Singhania (or somebody from his family) was there to attend the conference. Our minds started working overtime – "Singhania is from Kanpur. Perhaps we can play a Kanpur connection with him," we thought.

"Can we talk to Mr. Singhania?" we asked the guard.

He went in to check and returned with news that he is busy until noon.

"Okay, we will come back at noon," we said.

We strolled around the streets of Naini Taal empty stomach being agonized with the sights of people eating. At that time if we were given a

128

choice to spend a night with Zeenat Aman (the heart throb at that time) or eat an आलू पराठा, I am sure we would have opted for the later.

Returning to the hotel a little bit after noon, we learnt that Mr. Singhania just had his lunch and now he is enjoying his siesta.

"When will he be up?" we asked.

The guard went inside and brought with him Singhania's secretary.

"कौन हैं आप लोग? क्या बात है?" asked the secretary nervously.

"जी हम लोग IIT से हैं. Singhania साहब से मिलना है," we said very politely.
"IIT Kanpur?" he asked.
"जी हां,"
Perhaps the name IIT did the trick.
"वो ३ बजे उठेंगे. आप आपना नाम दे दीजिये. जब वो उठेंगे मैं उन्हें बता दूंगा," he said.
"बहुत बहुत धन्यवाद आपका. नमस्ते," we all said politely with folded hands and bowed heads.

For the next two hours we stayed within the sight of the guard playing in our minds what we were going to tell Mr. Singhania.

A plan was hatched.

Slightly after 3, the secretary came out.

"साहिब अब आपसे मिलेंगे," he said with a grin on his face.

As soon as we heard that we started to follow him. He turned around, paused, looked at us (and perhaps also smelled our body odor), and said, "आप बाहर ही रुकिये. मैं साहब को बाहर बुलाता हूं."

Within a few minutes comes out a bulky man in his thirties, about 5' 8", with a big belly, donning a silk कुर्ता पायजामा, and a thick gold chain around his toad-like neck. He looked rich and well fed.

"You guys are from IIT Kanpur?" he asked with a mild smile.

"Yes," we all said together feeling thankful to our institution for giving us this very important identity.

"What can I do for you?" he asked.

According to the plan, **Pr** was to impress him first with his eloquence on English speaking.

As rehearsed, he delivered flawlessly.

"Sir, we are caught up in a sticky situation. While we were cogitating about what to do about it, we learnt that you are in town."
"Way to go P," thought **Ma** and **As** without knowing what 'cogitating' meant.

"What sticky situation?" he asked.

"We came here yesterday for peregrination a couple of days ago. We were supposed to return back to IIT yesterday but then we realized that our wallet was stolen," said **Pr**.

It was not clear if the साहब knew what peregrination meant. But that was the idea – to confuse him so he wouldn't ask too many questions.

"That is too bad?" he said.

Ma jumped in, "I have called my father in Bombay (it used to be Bombay then, not Mumbai) who will be taking a flight to reach here soon, but it will be at least tomorrow before he can come here. If we don't make it back to IIT by tomorrow we will miss a very important meeting."

As soon as **Ma** completed his sentence, **Pr** butted in making sure to not give the साहब any time to think, "If you can loan us just enough dough for us to return back Kanpur, it will save our parents a lot of trouble. As soon as we go back, we promise we will return your money."

130

Pr's impeccable English, mixed with words that make most people scratch their heads, did the trick.

"How much do you need?" he asked.

We never expected it to be that easy, and hence, we never rehearsed this part. One of us blurted out (don't remember who it was), "I think 100 rupees should be enough."

Before we finished the sentence, the साहब digged into his silk kurta's pocket, and took out a stack of 50 rupee bills, and gave us two of those bills.

"Thank you very much sir. As soon as we reach Kanpur, we will return this money," said one of us.

He knew that we will never see him again because none of us bothered to get his business card or his mailing address before we parted.

As soon as the साहब went in, we felt like somebody had blown life into a carcass.

"We should have asked for more money," opined **As**.

"Shut the f..k up. We are in so much trouble because of your genius in Thermodynamics," **Pr** snapped.

The first thing we did was to have a good meal. We ordered मटन दो प्याजा, मलाई कोफ्ता, and तन्दूरी रोटी. It is hard to describe the feeling when we took our first bite – just unadulterated ecstasy, better than sex.

After the hearty meal, it was time to plan our return trip. With our tummies full and money in our pocket, it appeared that our troubles were over - not by a long shot. Our scooter had some more surprises for us. Yes, you guessed it - it refused to start even though its belly had enough gasoline in it.

We took it a mechanic who, after learning the abuse it had been subjected to, suggested another engine clean up. For another 40 rupees, he got the scooter roaring again. He strongly advised us that the scooter was old and its engine may not have enough muscle to take all three of us back to Kanpur.

We now had exactly 30 rupees with us. It was about 5 pm and we had to make some hard decisions before the darkness engulfed us again. It was decided that only two of us will ride the scooter and the third one will take a public transport. Since **As** did not know how to drive a scooter, he was given ten rupees and asked to find some creative ways to reach Kanpur. By default, the responsibility of taking the beat up scooter back to Kanpur fell on the shoulders of **Ma** and **Pr** with a total of 20 rupees in their pocket.

We don't know what happened to **As**. Till this day, we have never seen him. All we know is that he reached Kanpur safely the next day.

The rest of the story –

After we dropped **As** to a bus stand, we started our return journey. In order to save gasoline, we put the scooter in neutral, sat on it, and just let it roll downhill until we reached the plane. After that we drove for several hours while keeping an eye on the fuel indicator. We added ten rupees worth of gasoline to it. Now we had only ten rupees with us. After driving for some more time we noticed the fuel indicator needle kissing the empty mark. It was time to be creative again.

A plan was hatched.

It was about midnight. We saw, at a distance, a gas station on the side of the road. The layout of the gas station was kind of semicircular with entrance on one side and exit on the other. The gasoline filling point was in the middle of the semicircle. According to the plan, **Ma** dropped **Pr** at the entrance and drove straight to the filling point.

"पूरा भर दो," **Ma** instructed the attendant.

"बहुत अच्छा साहब," said the attendant as he opened the gas tank lid.

Meanwhile, according to the plan, **Pr** walked to the exit end of the gas station and sat there.

After topping the tank, the attendant said, "३२ रुपये साहब."

Ma pretended to look for his wallet. Not finding his wallet, he called out to **Pr** making sure that the attendant heard every word of the conversation,"मेरा बटुआ तुम्हारे पास है. ३२ रुपये दो आकर."

"मैं बहुत थक गया हूं. तुम यहां आकर ले जाओ," **Pr** yelled back while flashing the wallet.

"ये मज़ाक का टाईम नहीं है. जल्दी आकर पैसे दो," **Ma** replied, pretending to be frustrated as the attendant looked on.

Pr continued to sit, refusing to budge.

"तुमसे हम कह रहें हैं कि मुझमें बिलकुल ताकत नहीं है. यहां आकर पैसे ले जाओ," said **Pr** acting very tired.

"तुम यहां रुको. मैं अभी पैसे ले कर आता हूं," said **Ma** to the attendant as he kick started the scooter.

Attendant stood there confused while **Ma** drove to the exit side where **Pr** quickly hopped on to the back seat and we sped as fast as the scooter's pick-up would allow. It was too dark to see if the attendant ran after us. We rode for half an hour at top speed while **Pr** continued to look back to see if anybody was chasing them. It was all clear. We just successfully pulled our first heist. After driving for another couple of hours, we stopped at a roadside ढाबा and ate आलू पराठा with the lone ten rupees that we had on us. We were now feeling at the top of the world – an almost full tank of gas and satisfied tummies. We could almost smell the aroma of IIT. With this speed we will be there in about four hours. You may think that our troubles were over – NOT REALLY.

Fast forward to 3 hours.

We just entered the outskirts of Kanpur. The sight of Kanpur city lights at a distance appeared to be saying – Welcome home, my children. **Ma** glanced at the fuel gage. There was enough fuel in the tank. "We will be there in less than half an hour," he said to **Pr** sitting in the back. The thought of being back in the campus made **Pr** stretch his hands like Leonardo DiCaprio in Titanic tasting the breeze of freedom.

At a distance we saw a group of policemen sitting at the ledge of a small narrow bridge. As soon as we approached the bridge, they stood up swinging their batons.

"गाड़ी रोको," shouted one of them.

We stopped the scooter without fearing anything as we had done no wrong. The head honcho, दरोगा, approached us right in our face. If we didn't have our own body odor to fight off the stench of his bad breadth, he would have continued to bring his yellow teeth right into our faces.

"कहां से आ रहा है?" he growled, tapping his baton on to our shoulders.

We hadn't looked at ourselves in mirror for more than 3 days, but looking at each other we knew we looked no less ferocious than Sholay's Gabbar Singh.

"जी नैनी ताल से," said one of us meekly.

"कहां से?" he asked again with his voice raised to even higher decibels.

"जी नैनी ताल से," we said again.

"ये कहीं से डाका डाल के आ रहें हैं. तलाशी लो सालों की," he ordered his subordinates.

Two of the police men held us by our necks and brought us at the side of the road while the third one took the possession of the scooter. We

134

were probed deeply, intimately, and thoroughly. It may sound creepy but since every muscle of our body was aching so badly that the touch of another human being against our sore thighs felt like a gentle massage.

Then suddenly the man searching the scooter shouted, "साहब, शराब की दो खाली बोतलें मिली हैं."

"अरे मैं तो देख कर ही समझ गया था कि ये दोनो साले कोइ गुन्डे हैं," said the दरोगा, crowing on his genius in identifying criminals.

Luckily **As** was not there with us at that time because if he was we would have choked him to death for preventing us from throwing away the bottles.

"सच सच बता कि कहां डाका डाला है वरना तेरी बाडी में इतने छेद करूंगा कि कनफ्यूज़ हो जाओगे कि सांस कहां से लें और पादें कहां से," growled the दरोगा (he actually didn't say the last part, but we were sure he meant that).

"जी हम सच बता रहें हैं, हम नैनी ताल से ही आ रहे हैं," we pleaded.

"बन्द कर दो सालों को. ये साले लातों के भूत बातों से नहीं मांनेंगे," ordered the दरोगा.

As instructed, we were handcuffed and dragged to the nearby Police Thanaa.

The Thanaa incharge was a fat guy, about 5'1", in his forties, with a HUGE belly.

"ये क्या ले आये हो," he asked, sneering at us.

"साहब ने इनपे रात भर कड़ी नजर रखने को कहा है. वो इनसे सुबह बात करेंगे," said the policeman, handing over our leashes to the Thanaa incharge.

Right after that, the Thanaa incharge took out his double barrel rifle and put two fresh cartridges in each barrel, making sure that we saw it and we understood that these cartridges had our names written on them.

We sat there handcuffed on the floor with other prisoners.

"What are we going to do now?" **Ma** asked **Pr**.

"If we involve IIT administration into it we will be in a big trouble," said **Pr**.

"That's right. Do you know somebody in Kanpur who can vouch for us?" asked **Ma**.

"I was thinking about the same. My uncle lives in Kanpur. I think I should call him," said **Pr**.

"Will he flip out when he learns what we have been through?" asked **Ma**.

"He may, but he is kind of resourceful and a cool guy. I'll call him in the morning."

Well, to cut the long story short, **Pr**'s uncle arrived at about 9 am, took the possession of the scooter, got us out, and gave us some money to take the tempo to IIT. Our troubles didn't end yet; but the story is getting a bit too long, so I will end here.

We arrived at the campus and headed straight to our respective rooms.

It has been 35 years. Till this date after the 'Trip through Hell,' **Ma**, **Pr**, and **As** have never met, never talked on phone, never exchanged emails, none of us know where the others are.

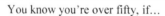

You know you're over fifty, if...

You are warned to slow down by your doctor instead of the police.

A few months after his marriage, **Jh** had a chance to come to Kanpur with wife in 1981. He decided to show her the IIT campus and share with her the memories of his IIT days. "What if we run into some of his classmates or his professors," she thought, "I must look my best." As **Jh** looked at her, who was in salwar suit and looking like a young girl, he could not take his eyes off her. "बहुत कमसिन लग रही हो, बिलकुल कालेज की लड़की की तरह," he said lustfully, pulling her closer to him. If they were not getting late, she would have probably let him continue with his advances. But at that moment seeing IIT campus was the only thing in her mind. "अभी नहीं वरना वहां के लिये देर हो जायेगी" she blushed. Patience being one of his virtues, **Jh** agreed to take the rain check.

He showed her several places in the campus. "See, this is the Library where I used to spend lot of time studying (?); that is the Swimming Pool where I perfected my swimming; these are the hostels where I spent many years, etc. Simultaneously, he narrated a few interesting experiences during his IIT days (of course, the goody goody ones only).

Finally, he took her to one of his most favorite places – the top of the Faculty Building. As he rode the elevator to the top floor, he told her that quite often, during summer evenings, he along with couple of his friends used to go to the terrace of F.B. and further climb via the iron ladder up to top of the Water Tank where they used to spend some time enjoying the breeze, watching the far away lights and chatting/bulling, filled with a feeling of being at the top of IIT/K (if not the "Topper"). Enthusiastically, he suggested to her to go to the same "top of IIT/K" and his wife gleefully agreed. So both of them climbed up to the top of the Water Tank where they sat enjoying the bird's eye view of the campus, the breeze, the solitude, and each other's company.

Their state of oblivion was suddenly disturbed by a loud tapping noise coming from the water tank. As they turned their head in the direction of the noise, they saw a burly looking security guard looking up at them.

"ऊपर तुम दोनो क्या कर रहे हो, नीचे उतरो," he shouted as if he had caught someone red-handed for a foul play.

Jh didn't think too much of it as he knew that the girl accompanying him was his legally married wife. He told her not to worry and that as soon as the guard knew the truth he will leave them alone. He helped her come down the tank.

"मैं IIT/K ka ex-student हूं और ये मेरी पत्नी है," replied Jh calmly.

"तो वहां क्या अपनी पत्नी के साथ honeymoon मना रहे हो?" said the guard sarcastically.

The tone of the guard's voice was a matter of concern for Jh. He again tried to reason with him, "मैं अपनी wife को IIT campus दिखाने लाया हूं."

But the guard seemed unconvinced. "अच्छा, तो यहां faculty building की छत पर और वो भी टंकी के ऊपर wife को दिखाने लायक क्या चीज है? मुझे तो यह लड़की तुम्हारी पत्नी नहीं लगती है. सच सच बता दो कि क्या चक्कर है वरना तुम दोनो को मेरे साथ Kalyanpur Police Chowki चलना होगा. फिर वहां दरोगा जी decide करेंगे कि कौन किसकी पत्नी है. वैसे भी एक लड़की के साथ टंकी के ऊपर चढ़ना risky भी है," said the guard.

At this point, Jh saw two crows perched on the water tank. "ये बताओ कि वो दोनो कौए वहां पर क्या कर रहे हैं?" he asked the guard, pointing towards the crows. The guard was taken aback by this diverting tactic of Jh.

Yet, seeing an angry & worried face of his wife, Jh now realized that although nothing adverse would finally happen, but considerable hassles & inconvenience would surely be faced if they had to go to the police station. So he again tried to convince the guard that he was an ex-student and that the 'girl' was actually his 'wife'. However, the guard was only partly convinced and still insisted to go to the Police Station.

The guard then decided to find out the 'truth' from the 'girl', keeping Jh away at an inaudible distance. "बेटी सच सच बता दो. ये तुम्हे यहां पर फुसला के तो नहीं लाया है? Police में जाने पर तुम्हारी भी बदनामी होगी. वैसे क्या तुम सही में इसकी पत्नी हो?"

She, however in her own way, succeeded in convincing the guard that she really was Jh's wife. It was then only, that the finally convinced guard dropped his insistence to go to the police and he also apologized to both **Jh** and his wife, who finally took a sigh of relief. But by this time, **Jh**'s wife was so exasperated that she refused to visit further places in the campus and both returned back to the city.

An advice from **Jh** – "Never travel with your wife, especially if she looks as कमसिन as mine, to a new place without marriage certificate in your pocket." Since then he has religiously been following this principle.

You know you're over fifty, if...

You keep a long pencil in your coat pocket if in case you are constipated.

140

30 yrs. later – You only live once

The originator of this off-the-wall fantasy was none other than Mohan – the fantasy of living like नवाबs, uninterrupted for at least a week. When Mohan floated this idea to a limited audience, Madhukar was quick to point out that Nawaabiat and being with your spouse are mutually exclusive (please identify yourself, if you disagree). This led to the crystallization of an idea of a trip to a nowhere-land minus spouses. It was then floated to a larger audience. Initially, about 12 of us were enthusiastic and gave their commitment to be part of the fantasy trip. But when it came the time to actually take the plunge, there were only six brave men standing – Vipul Agarawal from Kanpur, K.K. Shukla aka KK from Lucknow, Barid Mitra from Delhi, Deepak Saran from Mumbai, Mohan Arora from Kolkata, and Madhukar from USA - जो हमसे टकरायेगा, वो चूर चूर हो जायेगा - इंकलाब ज़िन्दाबाद!

The trip was mostly planned by Mohan, but other responsibilities such as music, junk food, games, playing cards, etc. were shared by the rest of the gang. The trip had excitement (गोली) written all over it right from the beginning. On his way to Delhi, Madhukar was stuck in London because all flights were cancelled due to a bad snow storm. Next day, after a lot of begging, he was given a flight to Delhi in a 'no name' carrier. As expected, all his suitcases, including the one containing the warm gear for the trip, were missing. He waited there for a day bitching to airline bosses, finally accepting the inevitable that his luggage will not arrive in time or it may never arrive. He bought another set of bare minimum clothes so he would not freeze to death in bone chilling temperatures at Kasol. Thanks to Vipul who brought lot of extra warm gears just for these kinds of emergencies.

All six of us (from now on, let's call us "six brave men" instead of "six idiots") assembled in a guest house in Delhi on Dec. 24. There were three rooms and six of us. KK proposed that we should use a secret balloting system to decide who is going to share room with whom. After this suggestion was laughed off, it was time for the next गोली. While the rest of the gang was drinking, yapping, and laughing, KK was frantically pacing the room. It turned out that KK had forgotten the combination to open his suitcase (another suitcase disaster). It was way past midnight and our flight was early in the morning. So the option to forcibly break open the suitcase and purchase another suitcase was out of question. While all this commotion was happening, Barid was sitting quietly staring at the ceiling. After doing mental calculations he proclaimed that there are only 999 possible permutations, and there is no choice but to try all of them sequentially until the right one is found. We had four hours to leave the guesthouse to catch our flight. Was there enough time to try all the permutations? To answer this question, we had to find the rate (dN/dt) of checking numbers. It was decided that KK will first try ten numbers while Deepak Saran will time him. Based on the rate calculated, it was estimated that we had barely enough time to try all the permutations. Thus without wasting any time, KK sat down with the suitcase on his lap and started with 111, 112, 113, ….. while the rest of the brave men stood around him in a circle each holding a glass filled with 100 Pipers and cheered him on. Vipul, from time to time, would remind KK the perils of skipping a number because the skipped number may be the right one. Well finally, KK hit the jackpot at number 884. He jumped with joy and hugged everybody while licking his sore fingers. He was very happy and immediately proceeded to the bathroom to reward himself – it was quite satisfying to see that he had not changed a bit from his IIT days.

There was only one hour left before we had to go the airport to catch our flight to Guntur. So instead of catching an hour of sleep, we decided to do what we went there to do, that is to be Nawaabs. So we continued drinking, yapping, cracking jokes, laughing…. We noticed that KK was pacing the room yet again. What now? "I can't find my glasses," announced KK. Mohan demanded the detailed description of the glasses so he could look for it. Like good comrades, all of us looked for his glasses.

When we could not locate it, Deepak asked KK – "KK, you are quite drunk. Is it possible that you may have flushed your glasses with your other bodily fluid in the toilet?" KK was not very amused with this suggestion but he still went to all three bathrooms and peeked into the toilets, just in case. Well to cut the long story short, it turned out that all this time his glasses were safely perched in his shirt pocket.

It was now clear to everybody that this trip was going to be full of गोलीs.

To our surprise we all made it to Kingfisher's counter in time. There we ran into Madhukar's wife and his daughter who had just arrived from US. There we learnt that like her husband she also arrived minus her four suitcases – clearly these two are made for each other.

Fast forward to our hotel in Kasol:

On reaching Kasol in our lodge - the first comment about the place coming out of Vipul was - क्या गां.. फाड़ू जगह है. पेड़ के नीचे पादो और नदी के किनारे हगो." Madhukar was visibly disturbed as he realized thereafter that the toilet paper roll that he had packed with great care was in his lost baggage. His long years in USA had de-skilled him in the art of use of ' लोटा - water - hand ' to do the finishing job. Since Vipul was paired with Madhukar, he volunteered to coach Madhukar on this art. Vipul outlined the procedure as:

- Before starting the cleaning operation put your thighs apart at 35-40 deg if the discharge is solid and 45-50 deg if it is sold-liquid mix. If it is completely liquid, don't worry about it, you are already clean.
- Hold a लोटा filled three fourth with water in your right hand by its neck and lower the palm of your left hand below your thighs at an angle of 15 deg to the horizontal keeping the tip of the fingers just below the centre of the area to be cleaned.
- Slowly pour water on your palm while simultaneously splashing the water on the area to be cleaned.
- From time to time probe the area with your fingers to assess the cleanliness.

- When satisfied, shake your bottom vigorously to remove the excess water. Pull up your pants.
- Don't forget to wash your hands with soap before exiting the bathroom.

Like a good student, Madhukar went inside the bathroom while Vipul waited outside. After about ten minutes, Madhukar came out walking like a pregnant penguin. "How was it?" asked Vipul curiously. Madhukar turned around. His blue jeans were completely wet from behind. "You didn't shake the excess water off, did you?" asked Vipul. Madhukar quietly nodded.

We had rented an entire top floor of a hotel. It was decided to be in pairs. Intentionally or unintentionally, it turned out that Mohan paired with Barid, Deepak paired with KK, and Vipul paired with Madhukar. After a couple of days, we heard some whispers coming from Deepak and KK's room. Since this was the first time KK lived without his better half, Deepak decided to fill this vacuum by taking up the most important of the spousal duties – nagging – he kept a strict watch on what KK ate. During our meal times, we would often hear Deepak commanding KK – "Don't eat omelet, it is not good for you. Eat boiled egg instead," or "don't eat the yellow part of the boiled egg," or "don't eat पराठा, there is too much grease in it, eat रोटी instead," or "don't use butter in your दाल," etc. etc. Perhaps, in the beginning KK appreciated this side of his caring roomy, but pretty soon he questioned –"Everybody else is eating like Nawaabs, why am I being permitted to eat only hospital food?" Rest of us tried to tell KK that Deepak was doing this because he is caring and concerned about your health. "Balls to my health," he snapped, visibly upset.

There is another incident that perhaps may have added to the love lost between them. KK had bought several pairs of warm socks for this trip. But when he needed them to fight the cold he could never find them in his suitcase. He suspected that perhaps those socks had found their way into Deepak's suitcase. He made Deepak look for them while he watched. His socks were nowhere to be found. That was it. He decided he didn't want to be Deepak's roomy anymore. He proposed that we should devise a system to select the pairing arrangement. So we made six chits – two marked with letter "A", two marked with letter "B", and two marked with letter "C". When each of us picked one chit, the arrangement was –

Deepak paired with Vipul, Mohan paired with KK, and Barid paired with Madhukar. Things went on for a couple of days without any major hick-ups.

The ordering of food was generally managed by Vipul which meant a nonstop gluttony. Accompanied with that was some food wastage. This was not taken lightly by Deepak. On one evening, while everybody was enjoying the dinner, Deepak decided to educate Vipul on hunger and poverty in the world. After Deepak finished his passionate lecture on the suffering around us, Vipul carelessly responded by quoting the well know हिन्दी saying, "दाने दाने पे लिखा है, खाने वाले का नाम." Before Deepak could react, Vipul continued while side glancing at the wastage on his plate, "It is not wastage. It is food for mice and cockroaches." This did it. Deepak blew his lid off. The discussion that had started in हिन्दी has now changed into a full-blown heated tirade in English. To aggravate the situation even further, Vipul threw in another googlie. "If you know so much about suffering in the world, tell me what the square root of 0.1 is." This was too much for Deepak – "How can such a serious discussion be brought to this level," he thundered. We were all afraid that if this argument between these two intellectuals was not roped in, the dishes were going to start flying soon. Well, finally the senses prevailed and these two guys soon realized how kiddish both of them had been. They calmed down and hugged and kissed each other.

Spilled Milk – what does it mean?

On another chilly night in the midst of our usual teen patti/booze session, a quite strange situation erupted which till today continues to bewilder all of us. Deepak, while recalling good old days with Barid, gently put his hand across Barid's shoulder. "Barid, do you remember when we went to see a movie," he asked affectionately hoping that like him Barid had also caged those intimate moments. Noticing the foggy look on Barid's face, he digged in deeper. "Remember the scene when the hero and heroine were cozying up in a bedroom," he said gleefully, "and then the scene changed to a glass of milk shaking violently eventually spilling the milk." Barid, who was still confused, faked a smile pretending that he also remembered the episode. Still not sure that Barid remembered this very emotional incident, Deepak pressed on, "Remember that I did not know what the spilling of milk meant? You were the one who explained to me the meaning of that, so I want to thank you for being my soul mate at IIT." The discomfort at Barid's face and his fake smile were clearly visible. Deepak, who till now was basking in the sweet memories, was visibly hurt by Barid's cool reaction to his warm gesture and we saw him suddenly visibly sad and dejected. Every one of us including Barid was taken aback - astonished, puzzled, amused and sad -all feelings mixed together. Barid helplessly looked at the rest of us as if trying to ask us if it was his fault that he had no recollection of the movie or the spilling-milk episode. Since none of us had ever seen a grown up man so emotionally moved like this (other than in Hindi movies), we thought it best to call it a day (night), say good night to each other and slip into our beds.

When Heat is in Short Supply, Be Creative

On another night while Deepak and KK were still roomies, Deepak came running to rest of us. He was clearly in a panic. "What happened?" we asked. "I think KK is not well and is shivering in his quilt. Mohan & Barid rushed to his room and found that KK was sleeping merrily. They woke him up and enquired. He was visibly upset on Deepak and explained that after slipping inside quilt he deliberately shivers for a few moments in order to make it warm quickly inside and that he was perfectly all right. Deepak did not like this explanation as his over caring instinct towards KK was perhaps hurt.

KK's Sweet Revenge on Deepak

Next day on the chilly morning, Deepak woke up early and started his morning chores. KK was on the bed half asleep keeping track of Deepak for his next attack on him. After Deepak had finished his basic chores he came out to get his clothes from his suitcase and before he was about to re-enter the bath room for his bath with only towel wrapped on, KK sprang from his bed saying 'बहुत जोर से लगी है' and giving a weird smile entered the bathroom before Deepak could react. Deepak stood out in cold scratching his head while his one hand on the wrapped towel ends (to make sure it did not drop down and reveal his family jewels). Deepak could do nothing but to shiver in the freezing cold outside. KK took more than his usual time with Deepak knocking at the bathroom door every five minutes. When KK came out he saw Deepak shivering in the quilt. A well planned sweet revenge.

Another Interesting Episode

Deepak, who had excluded himself from the trek journey to Pulga, remained back at the hotel at Kasol. As he was getting ready to shave, he found to his displeasure and anger, that KK, his roomy, had misplaced his 'use & throw' blade which was bought in the morning and kept by him on a table. So, he immediately rang KK on phone and expressing his anger enquired about the blade. KK, on the other hand, was very cool and did not take the matter as seriously as Deepak had expected from him. He advised Deepak not to worry at all and rather go downstairs and buy another one from the nearest shop. With no other option, Deepak did so and bought another blade, but by that time he was so much angered and furious that he decided not to shave the next day to protest KK's utter careless act and casual response.

After three days of non-stop 24-hour partying in Kasol we decided to head to Manali. We had agreed to start for Manali in morning by 10 am and reach Manali by 3 pm well before dusk – but the Nawaabs were intent on making a style statement – KK had to do yoga for the better part of the hour in the morning at 10 am…. Mohan had to complete his 3rd shitting…..

Deepak had to crib.....Vipul and Madhukar had to finish their third early morning beer... Barid had to have the series of marathon phone conversations with who knows whom.

We reached Manali at 6 pm when it was fairly dark. The first hotel was packed full without any vacancy. Deepak took up his role of the cribber very seriously and cribbed a bit more about rest of us not doing anything in time. By now the rest of the gang had learnt to ignore him. Mercifully the third hotel had just 3 rooms left and we gratefully accepted them. Barid's mannerism and appearance came really handy there. Without his winter cap, he looked like a recently retired seasoned दरोगा with his dark goggles. We used Barid to ensure that the hotel gives us the rooms and a discount which we got.

In order to ensure peace upon return to their homes, KK and Deepak went to Manali market to buy some stuff for their wives. It was quite late in the night and we did not hear from either of them. Then Mohan's phone rang – "I cannot find KK," said the voice at the other end. "Why don't you call his cell?" suggested Mohan. "I don't have his cell #," Deepak responded. Using his cell, Mohan played a role of a Global Positioning Satellite (GPS)-system and successfully connected these two. When they returned to our hotel rooms, they both were screaming at each other and trying to establish whose fault it was to disappear like that.

While shopping in Manali, KK had purchased some fruit wine which was the specialty of this region. Later on he would misplace them too. Till today he still wonders – "why do I lose things when I am with Deepak?"

On a lazy morning at breakfast table, Mohan proposed the idea of introducing WM 401 at IIT Kanpur. He would deliver complementary lectures for this particular course. In case you are wondering WM stands for "Wife Management". This would of course be a 4th year final semester course. He gave an hour lecture on the contents and the details of the proposed course.

Caught with his Pants Down

In order to keep every front happy, Madhukar, who had originally promised his wife that he would return back from our trip and join his family in Goa well in advance of New Year i.e. on 30th December, made a change in his plan to reach Goa on 31st December instead, after having gotten convinced from Mohan that it would be more enjoyable to be in company of six brave men by one more day [originally the brave men had planned to depart from Manali on 29th December]. As his ticket from Delhi to Goa was originally booked for 30th, so he tried to have it changed to 31st at the airport. He thought it prudent not to inform wife right then, but, rather tell her about the change towards the end of our trip making some convincing excuse. While he was standing at the ticket counter changing his return ticket from Manali to Goa for Dec. 31, he felt somebody tapping him on his shoulders. He turned around. One of his relatives was standing behind him. This relative is an airport official and was there to receive Madhukar's wife and daughter arriving from the USA. To show off his influence, he addressed the pretty lady at the counter by name, "सुनीता जी, अरे इनका काम जल्दी कर दीजिये." She smiled and quickly changed Madhukar's return ticket to 31st. Then the relative turned to Madhukar, and asked, "आप अपना टिकट क्यों change कर रहे हैं?" Realizing that the relative will soon be meeting with his wife, Madhukar had no choice but to request the relative to keep this a secret, "Please मेरी wife को मत बतायियेगा कि मैंने टिकट की date change करा दी है." The relative smiled slyly and agreed to keep his mouth shut. The relative was, however, quite God fearing, justice loving and believed in fair play. So in order to be just and fair to Madhukar's wife, he told her about Madhukar's act; not only this, he also told her that Madhukar had requested him not to tell her about it (in order to be just and fair to Madhukar too). And to be just and fair to himself as well, he also requested her not to tell Madhukar that he [relative] had told her all this.

We would not have come to know about all this, until it happened that Madhukar's mobile's talk value got exhausted when we were on our way back from Manali to Delhi in chartered mini bus and Madhukar requested Barid to arrange a talk with his wife on his [Barid's] cellphone. Barid obliged and after dialing to Madhukar's wife, handed over his set to Madhukar. Knowingly or unknowingly Barid kept it on the speaker-on mode and Madhukar went ahead talking with his wife without being aware

149

of it. So the rest of us were privy to the conversation from both sides. Initially Madhukar's wife, pretending innocence, enquired from him as to whether he was reaching Goa on 30th as agreed and Madhukar assured her that surely he would, and then started telling that certain unforeseen problems had started erupting which might force him to delay his arrival in Goa by one day, but still he was trying his best to keep up with the original schedule and so on. It was then we saw the color on Madhukar's face suddenly change as he was thereafter on receiving end and all his subsequent speaking on phone was just jheloing of googlies and bouncers from the other side. The rest of us were not in a position to decide whether to get amused by this conversation or have sympathy for Madhukar. Perhaps all of us might have faced such music at one time or the other in one form or the other.

Closing Remarks

Although wives were not part of this adventure, we must thank them from the deepest valleys of our heart for packing bags of delicious food. It went really well with beer and scotch. We also extend our thanks to Cellphone Services for not providing good services in the area so our better halves could not use the "electronic leash" to check on us every fifteen minutes.

 Friends, enjoy while you can because the day is not too far when

You will forget names,
then you will forget faces,
then you will forget to pull your zipper up,
then you will forget to pull your zipper down. ~ Leo Rosenberg.

That's not all...

CPSIA information can be obtained
at www.ICGtesting.com
Printed in the USA
BVOW09s2126311017
499169BV00008B/51/P